ACCOUNTING
FOR BUSINESS COMBINATIONS

A Practical and Empirical Comment

John C. Burton
Professor of Accounting and
Finance, Columbia University

sponsored by the
Financial Executives
Research Foundation

Accounting for Business Combinations
Copyright 1970

Financial Executives Research Foundation
50 West 44th Street, New York, N. Y. 10036

Library of Congress Catalog Card Number 70-141249
Printed in the United States of America

$5.00

First Printing

As the research arm of Financial Executives Institute, the basic objective of the Research Foundation is to sponsor fundamental research and publish authoritative material in the fields of business management with particular emphasis on the principles and practices of financial management and its evolving role in the management of business.

Publication of a research study should not be interpreted as constituting endorsement by the Board as a whole, or by individual Trustees.

JAN 7 1972

PROJECT ADVISORY COMMITTEE

Contents

Appendices

FOREWORD

This study marks a new departure for Financial Executives Research Foundation. Normally, the studies sponsored by the Foundation are long-range, in-depth projects to which a considerable amount of time has been devoted by the researcher.

This study by Professor Burton was initiated during the period in which the Accounting Principles Board was developing its Opinion on business combination accounting. Because the APB Opinion was imminent, severe time restraints were imposed upon Professor Burton. It was felt that if his study were to have practical value, it must be in the hands of the members of the Accounting Principles Board in time for their deliberations on the final Opinion.

Professor Burton completed his study under these constraints and a preliminary draft of the completed work was delivered to the APB in early June, 1970. We are confident that Professor Burton's work played an influential role in the subsequent development of APB Opinions No. 16 and 17.

It should be noted that throughout his work Professor Burton relates his findings to the preliminary APB Exposure Draft which was in circulation at the time of his research. Under these circumstances, it was deemed more appropriate to publish it as it was presented to the Accounting Principles Board earlier this year rather than to revise it extensively in the light of later developments.

As a result of his research Dr. Burton developed his own personal views on accounting for business combinations. These are set forth in the Addendum and are to be construed solely as his views and not those of the Project Advisory Committee or anyone else connected with the study.

To the many people who completed a questionnaire or those who were interviewed, the Trustees of the Research Foundation would like to express their grateful appreciation. To the researcher and to the Project Advisory Committee listed on Page iv, the Trustees give special acknowledgement for the combined constructive effort which has enabled this study to be completed.

We hope that Dr. Burton's work will receive careful and conscientious consideration by all those concerned with accounting for business combinations.

Donald P. Jones, President
FERF

PREFACE

THE RESEARCH STUDY which follows represents a research effort undertaken under extreme time pressure. The time span from the date work was commenced to the date the report was due amounted to ten weeks. The time available was limited to this short period since the research was started subsequent to the issuance of the Accounting Principles Board exposure draft of its proposed opinion on business combinations on February 23, 1970 and was undertaken primarily to provide data for the consideration of the Board prior to its June 24, 1970 meeting at which it proposed to act on the exposure draft. If the study was to have utility, the effect on the study of the time constraint had to be accepted.

At the same time, it must be recognized that meeting the time schedule had an impact on the extensiveness of the research. Several routine research steps had to be short cut. For example, two questionnaires were used in the study. Ordinarily such questionnaires would be pre-tested on a small

1

group of respondents and would be subjected to the careful scrutiny of colleagues and members of the project steering committee. This was done in only the most limited way and as a result some ambiguities passed through the screening and affected results. Similarly, a common research test would be to sample non-respondents to estimate bias in questionnaire responses. This process could not be accomplished satisfactorily in the time available.

While the study was undertaken originally to supply data to the Accounting Principles Board, the sponsors felt that subsequent publication would make the data gathered and the ideas presented available to others with an interest in continued study in the area. Additionally, publication would add some insights into the information available to the Board prior to the completion of its decision making process and as such would be useful to those with an interest in the historical development of generally accepted accounting principles. Finally, it seemed that many parts of the study would be of value to the academic world for use in the classroom.

Since the study did have as its focus the exposure draft published by the Accounting Principles Board, the researcher and the sponsors concurred that the utility of its publication would be greatly enhanced if it was published as soon as possible after the issuance of the Board's opinions on business combination accounting. Additionally, it was felt that to revise the entire study in the light of the final opinions issued would require rather extensive changes which would dilute the historical significance of the document. Accordingly, it was decided not to extend the empirical research nor to revise the text substantially, but to publish the study submitted to the Board after making limited editorial changes. The comments in the study relating to the Board's views, therefore, reflect the exposure draft dated February 23, 1970 and not the final opinions issued by the Board.

Although the research reported on is fairly extensive, it was clear from the first that the facts developed would not define a single and apparent solution to the problems of business combination accounting. Nevertheless, the data and the reasoning presented were useful to the Accounting Principles Board in seeking an improved pragmatic solution to a difficult problem, even though that solution did not coincide with the specific recommendations of this study.

Many people were involved in the research reported on herein. All deserve the great thanks of the author. Special mention must go to James Brigham who with the generous consent of his employer took a leave of absence from his regular work at Morgan Guaranty Trust Company to devote full time to this project as principal research associate. Without his intensive and effective labors and his insights into the problems involved the project could not have reached completion.

In addition, special thanks are due to Diane Heck, who participated in most of the research and to Leonard Kramer, Schuyler Lesher and John Ordman who worked on various parts of the study. Fred Meier, of the Bureau of Applied Social Research at Columbia, was enormously helpful in the many data processing tasks involved.

In the course of the research, four members of the Accounting Principles Board — George Catlett, Sidney Davidson, George Watt and Frank Weston — were interviewed and their thoughts and comments were very important in understanding the complexities of the issues and the decision process at work. Leonard Savoie of the American Institute of Certified Public Accountants was also helpful in this respect.

After the preliminary report was submitted, a number of colleagues were generous with their time in making helpful comments, many of which are reflected in the final manuscript. The contributions of Carl Nelson, Henry Reiling, Dean Eiteman and Frank Weston deserve specific mention. In addition, the Financial Executives Research Foundation Steering Committee which supervised the study made many significant contributions.

Finally, thanks must be given to the many corporate financial officers and chartered financial analysts who devoted their time and effort to supplying requested data and insights even when faced with unreasonably short deadlines for responses.

The author must also express his gratitude to the Financial Executives Research Foundation for setting him forth on this project and supplying the necessary resources to make the study possible.

JOHN C. BURTON

August 15, 1970

I

INTRODUCTION

IT IS GENERALLY AGREED that the application of generally accepted accounting principles to business combinations in recent years has led to some cases of reported results which did not lead to appropriate conclusions about the economic activity of the firm. Such financial reports were misleading to investors making decisions whether to buy or sell the equity securities of the reporting entity. Some of these situations have deservedly received considerable attention in the press.[1] The essence of these abuses has been that companies have been able to show growth in earnings and earnings per share in excess of real economic improvement.

---

[1] See, for example, "Dirty Pooling" and "Much Abused Goodwill" by Abraham Briloff in *Barron's*, "What are Earnings?" in *Forbes*.

In addition to some cases where it appears that economic reality has been distorted, it is also true that the business combinations area is one where alternative accounting principles exist to describe similar economic events which can be largely selected at the discretion of management to the detriment of comparability among reporting entities. There is empirical evidence drawn from a limited sample that companies are tending to select the accounting alternative which will maximize reported income within the range of acceptable accounting practice.[1]

It is clear that the Accounting Principles Board both has and feels a responsibility to deal with these problems. Accounting aberrations which present a misleading image of an economic entity reflect seriously upon the credibility of financial information and lower the respect of analysts and others for the reports of corporations. Comparability between companies is an important ingredient in the basic comparisons between investment alternatives that must be made by any analyst or investor.

The current Accounting Principles Board exposure draft[2] on the subject of business combinations demonstrates the Board's awareness of the need for the elimination of potential abuses of the criterion of fairness in reporting. At the same time, it goes considerably beyond this objective to prescribe a body of required accounting practice which represents a significant departure from current practice in many respects.

The need for these extensive changes in practice is not clear either in order to mend the abuses which current practice has permitted nor in terms of the inherent truth of the new theory developed. The Board's approach has been to take a completely new look at the subject of business combinations on the theory that if it finds the right answer, results reported in that framework must represent more useful information. No evidence has been presented by the Board, however, to indicate that the new conventions would produce more meaningful financial information for analysts, managers and other users. Even in purely theoretical terms, it is not intuitively obvious that the new principles represent the "right"

---

[1] Copeland, R.M. and Wojak, Joseph F., "Income Manipulations and the Purchase-Pooling Choice," *Journal of Accounting Research*, Autumn, 1969.

[2] Here and throughout this manuscript, "exposure draft" refers to the draft published by the Accounting Principles Board on February 23, 1970 which is included as Appendix C to this study. The final opinions (Opinions 16 and 17) of the Board differ in a number of respects from this exposure draft but since the draft served as the basis for this study and the empirical research was designed to test the rules outlined therein, the manuscript was not revised subsequent to the publication of the opinion to take changes into account.

answer. Indeed, it is quite clear that several of the crucial determinations made by the Board represent compromises rather than agreement on what the best procedures are.

This is not surprising when one recognizes that the Board today is essentially a quasi-legislative type of organization writing rules which must be followed by other parties. Many pressures are brought to bear by interested parties and the ultimate result is political in nature, reflecting the sum total of the various pressures and opinions absorbed by the Board. While such a legislative type procedure was not envisaged by the founders of the Board who saw it as an elite group of prophets interpreting truth from research, it is certainly arguable that the current approach which might be called "truth through negotiation" is the only practical one that could be adopted.

The end result of the process will generally lack theoretical purity but it will be an answer sufficient for use. As such it will serve a purpose as long as the Board has carefully considered its implications and its usefulness in giving a fair and understandable reflection of economic reality.

The purpose of this study is to consider the problem of business combination accounting in both theoretical and practical terms and in so doing to comment specifically on the APB exposure draft. The theory will be discussed with the objective of identifying the crucial areas of disagreement, but it seems apparent that the ultimate answer will not emerge from this discussion. This ground has been covered many times and is covered in the exposure draft, yet no recognition of truth has emerged except by assertion since theoretical answers are dependent upon the way in which problems are perceived. The conclusion of this study from reviewing the theory can only be that there is no one clearly correct conclusion.

If truth cannot be reached by introspection and revelation is rejected, the next best thing is to seek a sufficient answer. This requires an understanding of the many different answers that might be suggested and the implications of each, including the normal results of the accounting conventions applied in real situations as well as an understanding of the unusual situation where their application may create an unsatisfactory result. Additionally, the users of financial statements must be considered as their understanding of reported results is an important ingredient in the practicability of the ultimate solution.

If principles are to be determined on the basis of their practical results, objectives must be established so that suggested approach may be evaluated. The following objectives might be identified in setting accounting conventions in the business combinations area:

1. They must produce a result which is meaningful in the common sense terms which are the basis of traditional accounting. Thus they must not be inconsistent with what is generally understood to be the accounting approach.

2. They must help the user to perceive economic reality even though they may not produce a set of financial statements which directly measure such reality.

3. They must not permit situations in which obvious misstatements of economic realities exist.

4. They must be usable by all and used by all so that reported results of various entities may be meaningfully compared.

5. Criteria for selecting alternative principles must be reasonably precise so that similar economic events are reported consistently between firms.

In examining the practicality of the proposed opinion, the first step will be to examine the theory and identify crucial theoretical determinations. Then the various "abuses" which have been identified as associated with business combinations accounting will be identified and their frequency reported on. The adequacy of the exposure draft in dealing with them will be considered and any possible new "abuses" associated with it will be discussed. Third, the exposure draft will be considered in terms of the results which it will be likely to achieve. These will be approximated in part by examining the results which would have occurred had it been in effect in prior years. Finally, the views of analysts on business combination accounting will be reported and the impact of accounting methods on analysts' estimates of value will be estimated by use of an example.

When all these data are summarized, the right answer will still not have emerged with total clarity. It is hoped, however, that after consideration of the practical results presented, a better and more informed judgment can be made.

II

THE THEORY

The Basic Accounting Model

IT IS NOT SURPRISING that difficulty exists in accounting for business combinations because such transactions are among the most complex in the business world. This makes it almost inevitable that accounting which is based on a very simple approach to measurement will have difficulty in dealing satisfactorily with such transactions.

The basic accounting measurement model is not a systematically developed theoretical approach to business measurement based upon a careful appraisal of all possible complexities and uses for financial infor-

9

mation. Rather, accounting theory grew out of a common sense approach to reporting business events of a relatively routine nature. It was developed to deal with the simple trading enterprise and it was adapted without too much difficulty to the simple manufacturing firm, although even this step caused some trouble. The end result of the accounting process was a statement of results from the point of view of the owner of the enterprise.

Given these antecedents it is not surprising that accounting theory grew up on the basis of historical cost with a strong orientation toward certainty and objectivity of measurement. In the typical business firm a dollar of cost does produce a dollar of value and transactions take place sufficiently frequently to make it possible to await objective confirmation in the form of a completed transaction before recording an event on the books. In addition, since the model grew up through practice, it is not precisely defined and the same economic event may be described differently by different entities within the framework of acceptable accounting principles.

Accounting is at its least controversial, therefore, when it describes the simple economic event in the simple business firm. Cash goes out to purchase merchandise whose value is closely approximated by cost. Shortly thereafter, the merchandise is sold and cash returns to the firm. A matching of cash laid out (cost) and cash returned (revenue) measures the success of the firm in that operation. While a theoretical economist might raise questions based upon changing expectations and the time value of money, the businessman is quite content with the common sense matching process as a measure of economic success, and even the economist's measure would probably not differ materially in end result.

Application of the Model to Complex Transactions

As business transactions become more complex, however, the congruence between the common sense matching model of business operations and economic reality becomes less. The implicit cost-equals-value assumption of accounting breaks down when purchases are made of assets with uncertain future earning power, where costs are based on arbitrary allocations, where dollars spent for exploration and research yield benefits unrelated to dollar inputs and where the time between the instigation of a business event and its consummation expands adding both time and opportunity costs and uncertainty to the economic equation. In such cases, the relevance of the simple matching model is called into question as a means of useful economic measurement.

Two possible responses to such a situation exist. Either the basic objective, historical, matching approach can be discarded or amended in favor of some probabilistic value oriented system or the accountant can simply accept the economic inaccuracy of his measurements as the cost of maintaining his objective, simple and generally understood model. The latter is the approach for which he has generally opted although signs of change in the direction of a more economically oriented measurement model have been apparent in recent years.

Under the simple and objective approach, the real world, however complex, must be fitted into the simple model. This can be done by one or both of two methods. First, the accountant can define away the problem by claiming it does not exist. This means that he takes a complex transaction and transforms it for purposes of measurement into simple form so that it can be handled by the simple measurement model. This transformation makes it possible to describe events with the simple measurement model but it also leads to situations where economic reality is not reflected since no artificial transformation changes the economic essence of an event. The second means of dealing with a complex reality is to write a rule book which describes in detail how to account for each individual situation, thus substituting a known ritual in place of judgment in describing economic facts. The Accounting Principles Board has recently adopted both approaches in dealing with controversial areas of accounting. This is probably the only viable answer if the basic underpinnings of present financial reporting are to be maintained.

In order to understand the theoretical basis of the APB exposure draft, this process of simplification must be observed and the critical decision points identified. The choices made at these decision points define the ultimate conclusions reached in the exposure draft. The first step in this process is examination of some of the underlying principles behind financial statement presentation and understanding of their significance both from the standpoint of the real world and the simple accounting model.

UNDERLYING PRINCIPLES OF ACCOUNTING

Objectives of Accounting

The first decision point relates to the determination of the objectives of financial statements. One group of accounting theoreticians would identify the objective of financial statements as reflecting economic reality as closely as possible while a second group would look at the usefulness of results by various criteria rather than solely their relationship to economic truth.

Accountants and analysts have generally opted for the more certain answer in financial statements where a choice must be made between the more certain estimate and that most closely reflecting economic value. In addition, they have tended to prefer the answer which states assets at the lowest possible figure even when this requires a large charge against income not necessarily related to current operations. The financial community in general seems to prefer this approach, often failing to see the difference between good accounting and the accounting followed by good companies who can absorb large charges related to future revenues in current income without showing a decrease. There is a danger to this, however, since future results will not bear the cost which produced them and the matching model may thus be distorted. Today's conservatism may be tomorrow's overstatement.

It therefore must be recognized that the accountant's measure must be some form of proxy for economic reality if it is to be useful. Once it loses this characteristic, it may tend to mislead. Statements must help the reader to perceive reality even though the statements may not be a precise reflection of the reality itself.

To take one example, it is quite clear that when IBM ships a computer to a customer on short-term lease, it has generated economic value far in excess of a single month's or a single year's rental. Both past records and future estimates indicate that the computer is likely to be in place for a period of years and there is some statistical evidence as to what the distribution of time and revenue inflows would look like. Nevertheless, both analysts and accountants would almost unanimously resist the idea of recording the sales value of the computer shipped or the present value of the expected cash inflows as revenue during the period of shipment since the lease is cancellable and the future revenue stream uncertain and hard to measure. The conventional measure of revenue based on rentals as earned is both conservative and auditable and hence it is preferred. At the same time it can be empirically demonstrated that IBM stock values tend to fluctuate with shipments rather than with net income. This reinforces the argument that although the accountant is not reflecting economic reality and the analyst does not want him to, the analyst will try to base his valuation judgments upon economic reality rather than accounting statements.

As accounting techniques, statistical forecasting methods and understandable probabilistic models are developed, accounting principles may well evolve which increasingly reflect economic reality. In pension accounting, for example, a number of these approaches are used. At the present time, however, the vulnerability of such future oriented accounting principles to manipulative abuse and the lack of understanding likely to exist on the part of users of financial statements have led the accounting profession to adopt more certain criteria for recording events.

In choosing an accounting method for business combinations, therefore, it is not necessarily true that the method which most closely reflects economic reality is the one which will be most useful to analysts and others in making their decisions. The practical solution of an understandable and readily measurable result may be the present choice of users of financial information as compared to a more realistic but uncertain approach, as long as it does not obscure the economic facts involved.

Nature of the Entity

A second critical issue regarding financial statements is the nature of the entity being described. One approach views the firm as a group of assets being used to perform an economic function. While the source of these assets is shown on the balance sheet, the distinction between creditor and ownership interests is almost incidental, and liabilities and stockholders interest are generally combined as "equities." On the income statement, this approach reports the economic results of the firm's trading and investing activities. Revenues arising from the sale of assets or services are measured and the costs incurred in producing them are matched against the revenues to determine income. This can be identified as the operating view of the firm.

Another approach which differs in a number of respects is called the stockholder or ownership view of the firm. This views the business entity from the standpoint of the owner of the enterprise. On the balance sheet, stockholders' investment is a crucial figure representing the difference between assets and liabilities. Income under this approach represents the economic result of the stockholders' investment measured by the change in that investment (exclusive of capital contributions and withdrawals).

In many ways, there is little practical difference between these concepts. For some firms, the only change in stockholders' investment represents the operating results of the firm and hence identical income statements would result. When there is a charge for the use of debt capital, however, the operating approach would consider this capital withdrawal similar to a dividend, while the stockholder view would treat such a payment as interest expense and charge it against income. Similarly, the operating approach would not distinguish between minority and majority interest in the income of a subsidiary while the stockholder approach would take the view of the parent company shareholders and hence treat minority interest as a reduction in stockholder net income.

Traditional accounting has generally been ownership oriented rather than operating entity oriented, although there are some exceptions to this rule. In the case of minority interests mentioned above, for example, the stockholder approach would suggest excluding the minority share of assets, sales and expenses in a subsidiary so as to report solely from the point of view of the parent company stockholders. Actually, current practice is to include all assets, sales and expenses of the consolidated enterprise so as to show a complete operating picture and then convert net income and stockholders equity to a stockholder basis by subtracting a single figure representing the income applicable to the minority stockholders. Thus a combination of approaches is in fact used.

Although it it unimportant in many cases whether reporting is done from the point of view of the operating characteristics of the enterprise or from a stockholder viewpoint, in accounting for business combinations this difference has a significant impact. Many of the arguments raised in favor of pooling of interests accounting rest upon the operating concept of the firm.

The operating argument for pooling starts with the hypothesis that the balance sheet should show assets in such a manner as to reflect the operating characteristics of the enterprise most meaningfully and that the income statement should reflect the economic results of business activities during the reporting period.

The second and crucial stage in the argument suggests that the most meaningful way to value assets and to determine the costs that should be matched against revenues is to determine asset cost at any time when the operating characteristics of an asset are changed. When an individual productive asset is bought by a firm, it is placed in a new environment and thus assumes new operating characteristics. Thus a new cost becomes relevant. On the other hand, when a complete bundle of assets which have been operated together as a separate entity are absorbed together by a new owner without a change in operating characteristics, no new cost basis is required or appropriate.

If one adopts the stockholder view of the firm, however, this argument loses its relevance. The acquisition of assets by a new group of owners is sufficient basis for the revaluation of assets at the cost incurred to acquire them. Thus when the stockholders of the surviving entity represent a significantly different group than the previous owners of the assets involved, the stockholder orientation would lead toward the conclusion that the stockholders of the surviving entity had in fact paid when such a combination took place.

Nature of Assets

A final set of basic decisions about accounting principles must be made relating to the nature and valuation of assets which should be reflected on financial statements.

The first of these is whether or not the books should show only the specific identifiable assets acquired by the firm or whether recorded assets should include some measure of the economic worth of the firm over and above the value of its individual assets. It can certainly be argued that most firms have such an economic worth resulting from the excess of anticipated future earning power of the assets in their particular configuration and under the particular management over the earning power of the individual assets.

If such economic worth is to be recorded, a major problem of measurement would be created. Estimates by management or even by a qualified outsider would be subjective and subject to accusations of bias. An objective measurement technique could be based upon the stock market price of the firm's shares if a public market existed, but the relevance of this measure is subject to doubt due to supply and demand aberrations in the market place and the question as to whether the price of the marginal traded share multiplied by all shares outstanding is a reasonable measure of the fair market value of the firm as a whole.

The inclusion of such a value would create a large new asset whose relevance to the analytical evaluation of the firm is questionable.

The traditional answer of the accountant to this problem has been that such earning power value should be reflected on the books only when it has been acquired by an outside entity. The APB exposure draft is consistent with this approach. Whether or not it is logical to reflect the earning power value of part of an operating enterprise and not another part simply because the ownership of one has changed is a subject which has been debated extensively in the controversy over combination accounting. If one views the firm from the point of view of the stockholders of the continuing enterprise, it is reasonable to say that a transaction has occurred in regard to the entity acquired by the firm but not with respect to the continuing enterprise. Hence the two "goodwill" values can be differentiated although it may be argued in absolute terms that all such earning power value should be recorded. On the other hand, if the operating approach is adopted on the basis of the arguments outlined above, there is no apparent justification for recording one goodwill value but not the other.

Valuation of Assets

In addition to the problem as to the nature of assets which should be reflected on the financial statements, there are issues to be settled in the choice of a method of valuation. Should assets be recorded at their historical cost to the legal entity currently holding them, at historical cost to the economic entity with which they are now associated, at their historical cost when committed to their present operating use or at some measure of their current value? There are also significant questions as to whether cost, if it is to be used, should be based on a monetary or a purchasing power unit, but that is beyond the scope of this study since it is not directly related to the business combination problem.

The original accounting answer to this problem was to use historical cost to the legal entity. In recent years, the legal entity has become less important and the economic entity has been the crucial one in financial reporting. Thus cost incurred by the economic entity with which assets are currently associated has been increasingly the valuation basis used. Thus when a company becomes part of an economic entity through having its stock or net assets purchased, the cost paid by the acquiring entity becomes the reporting basis for the assets. When payment is made for stock and not for specific assets, that cost must be assigned equitably to individual assets in the process of consolidation.

The other approaches to valuation have not been generally used in public financial reporting. Cost when committed to current use has some support for public utility rate making purposes but has not frequently been advocated although the argument discussed above that values should be changed when operating characteristics of an asset change is a variant of this approach. Value accounting has been much discussed but little used.

The exposure draft suggests the revaluation of assets to a new cost basis when they have passed through a business combination and the nature of their ownership has changed in a significant fashion. Implicitly (through the 3 to 1 size test) the draft requires that when the ownership of assets changes by more than 75 per cent a revaluation should occur.

Opponents of the draft argue that a business combination does not represent a change in the essence of the business and hence should not be the basis for a revaluation of assets. They see a combination as a change in ownership similar to that which occurs when stockholders trade their stock. Therefore, they believe that the question of asset revaluation is not one which relates primarily to business combinations but rather is a broad subject which the accounting profession should deal with comprehensively instead of applying the concept to a narrow area with the resulting inconsistency in asset valuation.

ISSUES SPECIFIC TO BUSINESS COMBINATION ACCOUNTING

The next theoretical decision points are more specifically related to the business combination area. In many cases, however, the answers given will depend upon positions taken in solving the more general problems described above. The theoretical issues in business combination accounting can be divided effectively into two sections — those dealing with the nature of the event and those dealing with the nature of the asset created in the event.

Medium of Exchange

A first decision that must be made is whether the nature of what is exchanged affects the nature of the event. Is a business combination basically different when cash is exchanged as opposed to when stock or various hybrid securities are transferred? One group argues that the differences in what is exchanged represent basic differences in the nature of the event. They point out that when cash is issued there is no aggregate change in the total assets of the entity whereas when stock is issued, there is an aggregate increase in the assets under the control of the enterprise. In the second place, they suggest that an exchange of stock represents essentially a sharing of ownership interests including risks and the present value of future benefits, whereas a cash acquisition terminates the risk of ownership for the previous owners.

On the other side, the argument is presented that the issuance of stock to acquire another corporation reflects the incurrence of an opportunity cost which is just as real in economic terms as the disbursement of cash. These proponents point out that the corporation could have sold stock in the marketplace and used the cash to purchase the acquired company and they see no essential difference between the two transactions.

Some who hold this view will agree that when the amount of stock issued is very large in proportion to shares outstanding the opportunity cost argument loses validity because the ability to sell stock in such large quantities is doubtful. Even if such stock could be sold its value will depend on the earning power of the acquired company to a significant degree and thus it is not a good measure of cost to the original stockholders. Others feel that the proportion of shares issued has no relevance since they can point to numerous situations where corporations have been able to sell an enormous number of shares to the public at a price approximating current market value in order to complete an attractive acquisition.

A related issue that is frequently raised is whether an exchange of stock represents a business transaction of the sort that should be recorded on the books under conventional accounting methodology. Proponents of pooling of interests accounting argue that a business combination accomplished by an exchange of stock is in fact a deal between stockholders having nothing to do with the entity being reported on and as a matter of stock transfer it should not be recorded on the books.

This argument is embellished by identifying such a combination as a deal in which a mutual sharing of ownership takes place rather than the extinguishment of an interest or the creation of a new asset. The new stockholders have an interest in the assets of the old and vice-versa and the shareholders of both entities have given their approval to the deal, either explicitly or by authorizing the issuance of shares. If such a case can be established, the non-recording of the value of the shares issued on the books of the companies involved can be justified.

Others argue that in most cases it is clear that a transaction has occurred and from the viewpoint of the larger company's stockholders a price has been paid. In addition, they feel that when two operating entities come together, a basic change in operating characteristics as well as ownership has taken place and should be identified.

The Size of the Combining Companies

A second controversial issue which has been hotly debated in business combination accounting discussions is whether the size of the combining companies affects the nature of the event.

One side of this argument holds that when a very large and a very small firm combine, the result must inevitably be an acquisition of the smaller firm and a submersion of its interests in the larger enterprise. By the very size of the entities the nature of the transaction is defined. Even when the combination is accomplished by exchanging stock, the ownership proportion held by the acquired company stockholders is so small as to be insignificant. In such cases the large company emerges totally in control, and the small company may cease to be a meaningful economic entity. In addition, the value of the large company's stock will be independent of the acquired company and the opportunity cost discussed above can be relevantly measured.

At the same time, proponents of the size criterion argue that when two similar sized enterprises join forces through an exchange of stock, both companies' stockholders retain a significant interest in the business and both entities, now combined as one, continue to exist. Neither is submerged. This suggests that the two entities should merely be treated as a union of stockholder interests with no new basis of accountability for assets.

If the relevance of size is accepted, the problem of defining a size criterion must be faced. One approach is to leave this determination to the reporting entities based on their judgment in each individual case. Such an approach has the benefit of being flexible and avoiding arbitrariness, but in the past, managements have often seemed to allow their judgment to be based on the income result rather than on an appraisal of the economic realities and public accountants have made only limited attempts to constrain this tendency. This leads to inconsistencies that do not seem related to variations in economic reality, but rather to different methods of accounting for the same events. Thus while it is clear that no absolute truth exists in determining the right size criterion, a strong case can be made that if size is relevant, some dividing line should be prescribed in the interest of comparability and uniform application of accounting principles. Some have suggested that because there is no evidence supporting any single criterion, none should be established. They ask what magic can be found in a 25% criterion as opposed to 24% or 26%. The problem with this argument is that in the absence of some arbitrary criterion, no distinction need be made between 1% and 40%.

Even if it is agreed that a size criterion is desirable, the basis of the criterion and the level at which it should be established must be considered. The APB has suggested a criterion based on a fixed percentage of the number of shares of the combined entity. Large companies have argued eloquently that this discriminates against both very large and very small concerns. It should be possible to establish limits based upon absolute size or variable criteria depending on the level of other size measurements that would avoid the most dramatic cases of this discrimination, if it seemed desirable to do so.

The size criterion suggested in the exposure draft is quite restrictive and would sharply reduce the incidence of pooling of interests accounting. Our empirical study of its effect will be discussed in a later section of this report.

While size is considered very significant by some in determining the nature of a business combination, others find size totally irrelevant. They point out that when stock is exchanged, the shareholders of both enterprises obtain a proportionate interest in the assets and earning power of the combined entity, and as long as both interests remain proportionate, it cannot be asserted that one is submerged. The basic nature of the event, therefore, is not related to size.

In addition, the opponents of a size criterion argue that it is impossible to justify any criterion. They believe that the need to establish an arbitrary figure shows the basic illogic of using size. They also suggest that if an arbitrary level is prescribed, corporations will begin to design mergers with the objective of avoiding the size test and this will lead to new evils. If Company A acquires Company B and then acquires Company C, for example, none of the combinations may meet the test, while if B acquires C and then is acquired by A, both might qualify. In either case, the resulting entity is the combination of A, B and C, but the appearance of the entity's financial statements might be very different depending upon the order of merger.

Nature of the Assets Being Combined

A third issue not so fully discussed in the literature of combination accounting is whether the nature of the assets being combined affects the nature of the event. It has been suggested that when the assets of two combining firms are essentially similar and those of the smaller firm are simply inegrated into the operating assets of the larger, then the combination represents simply the acquisition of operating assets. This transaction is basically different from the situation where going businesses are combined with the intent of maintaining both as separate if related income streams.

Under this approach, the acquisition of operating assets by an entity would be the basis for revaluation at the price paid as if the assets had been obtained from an independent vendor, while the combination of independent earning streams would be a basically different event and would not require recognition of new values.

The problem with establishing this as a significant criterion in determining the nature of a combination is the difficulty in determining empirically what is being acquired. Lines will frequently be difficult to draw. While a conglomerate type merger can be easily identified, it is more difficult to deal with the acquisition of an entity with a complementary product which could be added to the product line of the acquiring company. Nevertheless, the question of what is being combined and the effect of that on determining the nature of the event deserves more comment than it has received in the literature.

Characteristics of Assets Created by Combination

The second set of theoretical decisions which must be made in business combination accounting are those associated with the assets acquired in business combinations. The problems of creation, valuation and amortization must all be considered.

The first question is whether in fact assets are created by a business combination, and whether such assets if created should be recorded on the financial statements. The creation of assets could be said to occur in a business combination either by the creation of economic wealth primarily through synergistic effects or by the legitimization of economic wealth previously created. Both elements are part of the "goodwill" generated by many combinations.

In determining whether assets are created, the question of why the business combination was accomplished must be determined. If its objective was to enable one company to acquire certain specific operating assets, no earning power would be acquired above the earning power of the particular assets and hence no new asset such as goodwill was created.

On the other hand, if the combination represented the acquisition of an earnings stream with assets being essentially incidental, a different answer might emerge. In such a circumstance, the value exchanged will generally exceed the value of the individual assets involved and this excess will represent the incremental earning power associated with the assets in a particular configuration under a particular management. In part this additional earning power might be created through the various economic benefits directly attributable to the merger and hence represent new wealth. In part, it might be attributable to the excess earning power already generated by the joining firm and merely legitimatized by the merger transaction.

In either event, when goodwill does exist the question of whether to record it on the books becomes important. This issue has already been discussed above in connection with the more general problem of asset valuation and recording. The conventional answer of the accountant is to record it if generated by another entity and acquired but not to put it on the books when it is self created. This answer means that only part of the goodwill of a combined entity will be reflected which is felt by some to be inconsistent. Others identify it as being consistent with the stockholder view of the firm which is a traditional assumption of generally accepted accounting principles.

In any event, goodwill value which was created over a period of many years and which may fluctuate sharply is reflected on the books at a particular time, thus enshrining its value at the date of the transaction.

An additional argument over the desirability of recording acquired goodwill is based on an analysis of the economic characteristics of the asset. It is suggested by some that the nature of this asset is so different that it confuses rather than enlightens readers of the balance sheet, and this confusion is increased when the income statement is affected as well.

There is a basic difference in the nature of goodwill in that it represents capitalized future earning power. The goodwill, if properly measured as the excess of price paid over the fair value of all assets acquired, is not the source of this future earning power but the result of it. This is a fundamental difference between it and the other assets of the business which are in fact the source of a future income stream. While both kinds of assets may be measured by the input cost of acquiring them, goodwill will not produce outputs while virtually all other assets will. Thus goodwill is not economically homogeneous with the other assets shown in that it is strictly a stockholder incurred cost rather than a source of future inflows. This fact has significant impact on the relevance of the matching model of income measurement as well as on the means of balance sheet presentation.

Valuation of Assets in Business Combinations

The second problem that must be dealt with in accounting for assets obtained in business combinations is the determination of the method of valuation to be used once it has been decided which assets will be reflected on the financial statements.

This is a special case of the problem of valuation discussed above. Normally, generally accepted accounting principles provide that financial statements will only reflect value when that value has been legitimatized by passage of the asset through a market transaction involving the firm.

When the principal things being obtained in a business combination are the specific producing assets of the acquired firm, a clear basis for revaluation exists if a transaction is assumed. The problem of allocating cost paid among a group of assets acquired together may create severe practical difficulties, however, both in terms of the cost of appraisal and its adequacy as a basis of allocation. If agreement is reached that a stockholder transaction does represent a market transaction involving the firm, even the issuance of stock for producing assets creates a basis for revaluation.

The valuation of goodwill poses additional problems. The conventional answer has been to appraise the value of the consideration given, subtract therefrom the fair value of the identifiable assets acquired, and record the remainder as goodwill. Where cash is disbursed in a combination, this method is conceptually straight-forward but significant practical difficulties arise in identifying and appraising the assets acquired. The assets must include intangible but identifiable items such as patents, franchises, contracts, customer and supplier lists, leases, trademarks, licenses and copyrights. Such assets are generally difficult to appraise. In too many cases, goodwill has simply been measured as the difference between cost and book value due to the difficulty of identifying and determining the fair value of all assets acquired.

Where stock is given, however, valuation problems arise in both sides of the equation. The most conventional approach to valuing stock issued is to multiply number of shares times market value on the date when the parties agree upon the transaction. Numerous questions have been raised, however, about the meaningfulness of market value both on a particular date and in general terms. Those who feel unhappy about market valuation point out that value at a given date represents merely the opinion of those who are trading the stock who represent a miniscule proportion of the stockholders. In addition, it is pointed out that market value is affected by a great many intangibles including the optimism or pessimism of the market place at any point in time which may be quite independent of the firm's activities.

The exposure draft suggests that "market value for a reasonable period before and after the date the terms of acquisition are agreed to and announced should be considered." This would allow some averaging to avoid short run market effects. Some question may be raised as to why market value after the terms are agreed upon should be considered since, in a major acquisition, this market value may be affected by anticipations of the performance of the acquired company. Hence the cost figure reported would not represent the cost from the point of view of the acquiring stockholders, which is the basis for using the purchase approach.

An additional question arises as to the adequacy of current stock market value in measuring opportunity cost. A significant discount might have to be taken against current market value to sell a large number of shares in the public market place and a substantial underwriting commission and offering expenses paid. Therefore, a discounted value may be more appropriate. This discount becomes larger as the floating supply of shares outstanding decreases. These various difficulties of measurement lead some to conclude that the market price of the stock is not a sufficiently accurate measure of fair market value since day to day changes in subjective investor expectations about the future as well as the other factors mentioned may have disproportionate impacts that should not be recorded on the books for posterity. While the basic philosophy of measurement on the basis of cost implies cost determination at a single point in time, in the case of most operating assets material day to day fluctuations in cost seldom occur and accordingly the cost equal value assumption implicit in the cost convention tends to hold over a longer period of time than is the case with stock market determined goodwill.

In criticizing market value, critics have also pointed out that most stock for stock exchanges are based on the relative selling prices of the two stocks involved and the relationship of these prices to earnings. Thus the market price and the price/earnings ratio of the acquired company will have a significant impact on the price paid. In measuring goodwill, however, only the price of the acquiring company's stock is used. Thus in a period when that stock sells for a high multiple, a company may be willing to pay a higher multiple of earnings and a higher premium over asset value to complete a merger and more goodwill would be recorded than in another merger essentially similar but based on an exchange where lower market multiples existed for both companies. If, for example, one company's stock was selling at $60 (40 times earnings) and the second company's at $20 (20 times earnings), approximately a 3 to 1 exchange ratio might be agreed upon. If the market price of the two stocks declined to $45 and $15 respectively due to a general market deterioration, the exchange ratio might be expected to remain the same if the merger took place and the proportionate sharing of earning power would be identical, but in the former case recorded goodwill would be much higher since it is computed as the difference between the acquiring company's stock value and the value of assets acquired which is largely independent of the market value of stock. It can therefore be suggested that the more speculative the market level, the more goodwill is recorded while at the same time the likelihood that such goodwill will continue to reflect economic value is reduced.

Amortization of Asset Cost

If an asset has been created and recorded, the final decision that must be made is what should happen to the asset cost. This determination of course relates closely to the concept of the nature of the asset which has been developed above. If one views the asset as being similar to the other assets of the business acquired for a defined cost and if one is willing to conclude that the value created will not have indefinite life, one is led inexorably to the conclusion expounded by the exposure draft that it should be amortized by a series of systematic expense charges prior to the determination of net income for stockholders.

This view is an example of the necessarily simplistic approach required to fit complex transactions into the accountant's one dimensional measurement model. The asset goodwill differs significantly from the conventional operating asset and its length of life is highly uncertain compared to an asset which can be described in terms of its operating characteristics. By assuming away these differences and forcing the facts into the model, the congruence between the accounting model and economic reality is jeopardized.

Even if it is agreed that goodwill should be amortized, however, the conclusion of the exposure draft that these charges should normally be on a straight line basis over 40 years by no means follows inexorably from the determination that it should be amortized. While it is true that the draft permits other methods where the corporation can demonstrate its appropriateness, it seems likely that 40 year straight line amortization will be used in most companies. A good case can be made that if the asset relates to earning power it should be amortized on the basis of some proportion of earnings rather than on a straight line basis over an arbitrary time period. It might also be argued that since goodwill is based on the present value of an earnings stream, the amortization pattern should take into account the fact that more is paid for a dollar of earnings in the early years following acquisition than for later earnings.

If the reader is not willing to accept the simplistic view of goodwill described above, it can be concluded that the amortization of goodwill as a cost against operating income may result in an understatement of operating results compared to the economic reality involved rather than in a fairer presentation of results.

One argument along these lines relates to the assumption that goodwill does not have indefinite life. Proponents admit that the purchased goodwill does not have indefinite life due to the discounting process which limits the worth of future earnings, but they point out that expenditures are being made and charged to expense annually in order to maintain that earning power, and thus the asset is being replenished annually. Under these conditions, the amortization of goodwill would represent a double counting of expense unless those costs spent to maintain earning power were capitalized at the same time. Since it is very difficult to identify these costs specifically, those who present this reasoning suggest that the non-amortization of goodwill is a more practical method of noting this effect.

A second group of arguments for the non-amortization of goodwill rest for their support on the basic difference between goodwill and other assets. If goodwill is different in a significant way, its amortization will create an income statement item which is of a different nature than other costs and which cannot be combined meaningfully with them. Thus an income statement including amortization will show an apples-and-oranges effect since amortization of goodwill represents an allocation of the cost of earning power while the other items in the income statement describe the sources of the earnings. Thus the economic activities of the firm are obscured by the inclusion of an expense charge not relating to those activities.

If goodwill is not to be amortized as a charge against income, some decision must be made as to what to do with it. Permanent capitalization is one solution, although a number of accountants are uncomfortable about a highly material asset continually growing as new acquisitions are made. In time, such an asset might come to dominate the balance sheet of merger minded companies and users might then be less able to observe the operating characteristics of the firm.

Another approach might call for the gradual extinguishment of the asset in some fashion that does not affect income measurement. This would almost inevitably require some revision of the principles outlined in APB Opinion 9, since some reduction of an equity account would have to be made.

A third approach is the one suggested by Accounting Research Study No. 10. The authors of that study recommend the direct charge-off of goodwill to Retained Earnings at the date of acquisition. This conclusion follows logically from the statement that the asset is not one that should be booked but if it is felt that the asset should be recorded its disposition should be directly against stockholder equity. However, this seems an unsatisfactory approach as well.

In the final analysis, then, there is probably no way to amortize goodwill in conformity with generally accepted accounting principles today if it is felt that this is an asset of such different character that its extinguishment should not be flowed through income. Any solution will require some modifications of today's conventional presentation of financial statements.

Summary

As we suggested earlier, the conclusion of this discussion of accounting theory related to business combinations remains that no firm conclusion is possible. The basic answers depend upon how you look at the problems and in such a situation different perceptions do lead to different presentations.

It must also be recognized, however, that there are costs to the availability of multiple accounting procedures. The benefit of consistent and comparable treatment of business combinations is considerable, and therefore there are strong arguments in finding a solution which everyone uses and understands even if everyone does not agree that it is ideal. In the absence of a theoretical imperative this requires a look at the practical results of various rules which could be imposed to see whether or not they meet the needs of users of financial information. It is to this we next turn.

III

THE SAMPLE

IF PRACTICALITY RATHER THAN THEORETICAL MAGNIFICENCE is to lead us toward a solution to business combination accounting, a first step is clearly to examine the real world. This is required both to understand the dimensions of the problem, to learn the deficiencies which exist in current practice and to test proposed solutions in a life like laboratory.

Ideally, an exhaustive census of all business combinations which had an individual or cumulative material effect on the financial statements of the surviving economic entity would be taken and studied, but constraints of time, budget and data availability precluded this approach. Instead, a sample was selected representing all mergers of industrial concerns in the calendar year 1967. This year was chosen because it was one of high stock market levels and merger activity, it was recent enough to encompass substantially all the accounting principles now in use, including APB Opinion No. 9 which had a material effect on income and earnings per share reporting, and it was the most recent year which could be selected for which results subsequent to the merger would be available.

The source of the sample was the list compiled by the National Industrial Conference Board which included all mergers of industrial concerns reported in *Moody's Industrials, Standard Corporation News, The Wall Street Journal, The New York Times* and the *Commercial and Financial Chronicle.*

The company listed as the acquirer in substantially all combinations listed was sent a questionnaire asking for extensive data on the business combination. (A copy of the questionnaire is attached as Appendix A.) We used a questionnaire rather than seeking published information both because compilation of the data from published sources would be too time

29

consuming and because much of the information sought in the study was unpublished. All respondents were assured anonymity.

The response to the questionnaire was not as great as had been hoped. Because of the time pressure involved we were able to give the companies only ten days to complete the questionnaire and return it. This, together with the confidential nature of some of the data requested, undoubtedly contributed to the relatively low response. Questionnaires were mailed to 1,119 companies representing 1,832 combinations. 224 companies involving 313 business combinations responded in one form or another. 191 of the questionnaires returned were substantially completed. A breakdown of responses to the questionnaire is given in the table below.

Table 1   Responses to the Questionnaire

	Individual Combinations	Individual Companies
Total Questionnaires Mailed	1832	1119
Total Responses	313	224
Completed Questionnaire	191	123
Did not complete questionnaire —Not a business combination*	31	28
—Insignificant acquisition	43	29
—Miscellaneous negative responses	48	44

*e.g., purchase of selected assets, purchase of product line, etc.

Since a number of respondents indicated that the acquisition listed on our questionnaire was not a real business combination but the purchase of limited assets or a less than majority interest, it was decided to examine the total National Industrial Conference Board list to see which of the combinations listed were not combinations of complete business entities and hence should be eliminated from our sample. In so doing, the acquisition of a complete division or subsidiary was included as a combination but the purchase of a plant, a product line, other limited assets or a minority interest was excluded. By this process, the total group of combinations was reduced from 1,832 to 1,603 for purposes of appraising response.

In addition to the questionnaire response, data was gathered on a sample of business combinations from the non-respondent group. We selected the 150 mergers in which the acquired company was a complete independent corporation whose stock was publicly traded prior to the combination. We drew our information from published sources including listing applications, proxy statements, annual reports, and financial publications. We recognized that this would be a highly biased sample in favor of large combinations but we felt that studying this group would in itself have some benefit. Of the 150 combinations in the original sample, we were able to gather meaningful information on 85. We were not able to gather sufficient information on 65 of the combinations either because the information was not included in sources at our disposal or because vital parts of the information were not disclosed by the corporation involved in the combination.

Table 2 below summarizes the responses to our questionnaire and our research in published data. From these data, it is clear that our responses are significantly greater from large acquiring companies than from small. The addition of published data further increases the tendency of our sample to emphasize large entities.

Table 2   Summary of Questionnaire Responses and Other Combinations Analyzed Classified by Asset Size

Asset Size of Acquiring Company ($000)	Number of Combinations	Respondents to Questionnaire No.	% Response	Combinations Analyzed from Published Data	Total Combinations Examined No.	% of Combination
No public information*	39	0	0.0%	0	0	0.0%
0 - $25,000	617	32	5.2	13	45	7.4
$ 25,001 - $50,000	242	22	9.1	7	29	12.0
$ 50,001 - $100,000	224	19	8.5	19	38	17.0
$100,001 - $200,000	202	38	18.8	20	58	28.7
$200,001 - $1,000,000	220	54	39.4	25	79	35.9
over $1 billion	59	26	44.1	1	27	45.8
	1,603	191		85	276	

*Four responses were received from a total of 43 acquiring companies whose stock is not publicly traded. These were classified in their appropriate size classes to make the size data as complete as possible.

The final step in studying non-respondents was to examine companies on which we had neither received nor collected data. Constraints of time prevented a thorough study of this group, but since the National Industrial Conference Board list which was the source of our sample provided estimated asset sizes of acquired and acquiring companies listed, we were able to obtain some indication of the size of these merger transactions.

Table 3 gives the distributions of the asset size of the individual companies which made acquisitions and of the asset size of the acquiring and acquired companies in each business combination. For comparison, similar distributions are given for our sample of 191 business combinations.

Table 3   Distribution of Asset Size of Respondents and Non-Respondents to the Questionnaire

	DISTRIBUTION FOR EACH COMBINATION				DISTRIBUTION FOR EACH ACQUIRING COMPANY	
	Acquiring Company		Acquired Company			
	Non-Respondents	Respondents	Non-Respondents	Respondents	Non-Respondents	Respondents
Privately Held Companies	8.4%	2.1%	94.2%	82.7%	14.5%	3.3%
Asset size not available	8.4%	2.1%	74.7%	33.5%	14.5%	3.3%
Asset size estimated (in thousands)						
$ 0 to $ 500			7.5	7.9		
$ 501 to $ 1,000			4.5	6.8		
over $1,000			7.5	34.6		
Publicly Held Companies	91.6%	97.9%	5.8%	17.3%	85.5%	96.7%
Asset size (in thousands)						
$ 0 to $ 1,000	23.3%	7.5%	3.7%	5.8%	24.7%	10.5%
$ 1,001 to $ 25,000	18.1	7.5	1.0	3.1	18.6	10.5
$ 25,001 to $ 50,000	15.2	10.8	0.4	2.1	13.2	7.0
$ 50,001 to $ 100,000	13.5	9.9	0.3	1.6	11.2	10.5
$100,001 to $ 200,000	9.7	20.7	0.2	3.1	6.5	20.6
$200,001 to $1,000,000	9.5	31.3	0.3	1.6	9.5	27.1
over $1,000,000	2.3	10.2	0.0	0.0	1.7	10.5

The asset sizes given in the NICB list are taken either from *Moody's Industrial Manual* where available or from *Thomas Register*. Where the asset sizes were shown as estimated or not available, we assumed that the corporation was not publicly held. Comparisons between the non-respondents and the questionnaire sample reveal that the questionnaire sample contains a higher percentage of both publicly held acquiring companies and publicly held acquired companies. Also, the acquiring and the acquired companies in the questionnaire sample are generally larger in terms of asset size than those in the group of non-respondents. This is only natural because the larger, publicly held companies are more likely to disclose the type of information asked for in our questionnaire. Further, companies are more likely to fill in questionnaires for the larger, more significant combinations than for the smaller, less significant ones.

From these tests, the inference cannot be drawn that our sample is without bias nor can we measure precisely what bias exists. It is also true that there was no audit of questionnaire responses so that the data reported to us were not independently verified. Nevertheless, we consider our sample of 191 respondents to be a reasonably representative group even if somewhat biased toward the larger more significant acquisitions. To the extent that it is so biased, the larger and more important combinations will be more fully examined. We feel that the inferences we draw from examining this group should hold true for significant business combinations in general.

For purposes of analysis, the combinations for which we do have information will be divided into three groups which will be alternatively examined depending upon the nature of the test. The first group consists of the 191 business combinations for which we received a completed questionnaire. From this group we will draw conclusions about business combinations in general. Tables 4 and 5 provide some data about the characteristics of the combinations in this sample.

As is indicated in Table 4, the common stock of 78% of the acquiring companies in this group was listed on the New York Stock Exchange; only 2% of the acquiring companies' stock was not publicly traded. This is in sharp contrast to the acquired companies, 81% of whose stock was not publicly traded.

Correspondingly, measured by either net income or sales or total assets, the mean size of the acquiring company was about 20 times greater than the mean size of the acquired company. As might have been expected, the mean size of the acquired companies in pooling transactions was about

Table 4 Characteristics of Business Combinations of 191 Respondents

(Dollar amounts in thousands)

Acquiring Companies

	Combinations Accounted for as poolings	Combinations Accounted for as purchases	Total (Includes part purchase, part pooling)
Common Stock			
Listed on New York Stock Exchange	84	62	148
Listed on American Stock Exchange	6	7	14
Traded over the counter	6	17	23
Not publicly traded	1	3	4
Purpose of the Acquisition			
1. Diversification	36	26	64
2. Acquisition of a related complete business to operated as a separate entity	40	29	70
3. Acquisition of assets, products or talents	19	31	50
4. Other	1	4	5
Consideration given in the exchange(*)			
Newly issued Common	65	16	83
Treasury stock acquired within one year of merger	3	0	4
Treasury stock acquired prior to one year from date of merger	6	7	13
Convertible Preferred Stock	27	3	31
Convertible Debt	1	2	3
Debt with Warrants	0	0	0
Other Preferred Stock	2	3	5
Straight Debt	0	8	8
Warrants & Options	3	0	3
Cash	3	60	65
Net Income in year mean	$ 29,498	$ 20,138	$ 25,325
prior to acquisition median	10,448	10,855	10,658
Sales in year prior mean	456,722	300,494	387,066
to acquisition median	220,642	177,920	199,772
Total Assets at year end mean	460,744	342.910	407,456
prior to acquisition median	160,721	138,540	146,270

Acquired Companies

Common Stock			
Listed on New York Stock Exchange	11	2	14
Listed on American Stock Exchange	6	1	7
Traded over the counter	9	2	12
Not publicly traded	71	82	154
Net Income in year mean	$ 1,965	$ 344	$ 1,387
prior to acquisition median	537	136	346
Sales in year prior mean	35,890	11,542	27,585
to acquisition median	7,844	5,957	7,000
Total Assets at year end mean	29,298	8,914	21,857
prior to acquisition median	4,447	2,874	3,539

*Totals do not add since more than one kind of consideration was given in several exchanges.

3 times as large as the acquired companies in purchases. In combinations with larger companies, the acquiring companies have more incentive to give stock and to take the benefits of pooling than in combinations with smaller companies.

The purpose of 79% of the combinations where the company was acquired as a pooling of interests was to acquire a complete company to be operated as a largely separate entity as compared with 61% of the purchases. More than one third of the purchased companies were acquired to obtain a product line or some assets such as a plant.

In the sample, there were 123 individual companies that had acquisitions during 1967. Table 5 shows the trend in the total number of combinations entered into by these companies and how they were accounted for during the 1966-1969 period.

Table 5   Business Combinations of 123 Sample Companies, 1966-1969

	1966	1967	1968	1969	Rate of Growth
Total number of Combinations	161	271	333	353	21.4%
Number accounted for as a:					
Pooling	70	125	173	179	26.5%
Purchase	89	139	156	163	16.3%
Part Purchase,, Part Pooling	2	7	4	4	—

The number of combinations increased substantially over the four year period, growing at a compound rate of 21.4%. The number of combinations accounted for as a pooling had a 26.5% growth rate compared with the 16.3% growth rate of purchases showing a trend toward pooling. In 1969, the rate of growth for all combinations and accounting methods slackened considerably, probably reflecting the weakening stock market.

The second group consists of 119 business combinations in which the acquired company was publicly held. This group is composed of the 85 combinations for which we gathered data ourselves and 33 combinations from Group 1. Of the 119 combinations, 90 were accounted for as poolings, 24 as purchases, and 5 as part purchase, part poolings. The results of our analysis of this group will apply in general only to large business combinations in which both parties are publicly held.

The final group is the total sample of 276 business combinations of which 162 were accounted for as poolings, 108 as purchases, and 6 as part purchase, part poolings.

Summary

For purposes of empirical study, a sample of business combinations was required. Mergers of industrial companies in 1967 were the sample used. The listing of mergers developed by the National Industrial Conference Board was the basis of the sample. This year was selected because it was one of high merger activity and it was the most current year for which information subsequent to the merger could be gathered and analyzed.

One of the most significant characteristics of combinations to emerge from a study of the sample was the disparate sizes of companies involved. In most cases, acquired companies were small and privately held prior to the combination. Only a relatively small proportion of the combinations involved two publicly held enterprises.

The responses to our questionnaire survey were biased toward large combinations. In addition, our examination of additional mergers based on public information was designed to obtain data about large and significant combinations. Our results therefore do not represent an unbiased sample of the population sampled but they do give a good approximation of the characteristics of the most significant mergers which are the ones about which we are most concerned.

IV

"ABUSES" IN BUSINESS
COMBINATION REPORTING

IN THE PRACTICAL WORLD OF ACCOUNTING PRINCIPLES, change should take place when it can be demonstrated that current practice is deficient. Since any change in principles requires a considerable educational effort and in the short run tends to reduce the understandability of statements to the average user, it should not be undertaken unless it can be demonstrated that it represents a significant improvement in the meaningfulness of reports or consistency among them.

A logical starting point in the search for practical principles of business combination accounting is therefore an examination of the various situations which have been considered to represent deficient reporting practices. These cases will be identified and reviewed first to

37

see in what sense they may be characterized as abuses and second to determine whether they are primarily related to the business combination problem or are more basic.

After this analysis, the sample of mergers will be surveyed to determine the extent to which these abuses occur and the exposure draft will be analyzed to judge its success in correcting the reporting deficiency. In using the sample to judge the incidence of abuses, it must be recognized that there is a probability of bias in the sample, particularly in areas where there is general agreement that a particular reporting practice is subject to criticism. Companies that used acceptable accounting principles to overstate economic results are probably less likely to respond to a questionnaire than those who did not.

Reporting abuses that have been described as associated with business combinations can be divided into three major categories. The first are cases of inadequate disclosure for purposes of adequate analysis of a company; second are situations where the application of generally accepted accounting principles has resulted in a mis-statement of enterprise position and results in combinations; and the third are examples in which accounting inconsistencies among companies have been noted. These categories will be dealt with in turn.

I. Inadequate Disclosure

1. Failure to Give Adequate Information About Combined Entities Prior to Combination

One complaint in regard to the adequacy of disclosure has been that corporations do not give sufficient information about acquired or combined entities to enable the analyst to distinguish between that which is happening to the original entity and that which is simply a function of a business combination. This is considered to be an abuse in the sense that it makes more difficult the task of forecasting the continued growth of the enterprise. The survey of analysts described below frequently elicited the response that growth through merger and growth through operating improvement were insufficiently differentiated in published financial information.

Various forms of disclosure inadequacies were observed in the sample. In some cases, prior year reports have not been restated when the combination was accounted for as a pooling, on the grounds of immateriality. When companies were purchased, performance prior to the date of purchase and pro forma financial statements were seldom presented.

The following table indicates disclosure practices followed by the sample companies:

Table 6   Disclosure of Pre-merger Results

	Combinations Accounted for as:	
	Pooling of Interests	*Purchase*
Restatement of Prior Year statements	87.7%	0%
Disclosure of pro forma data or prior year's income of acquired company	—	5.6%

The exposure draft seems effective in mending these deficiencies in disclosure. The disclosure requirements in connection with purchases call for footnote disclosure of the results of operations both for the current period and the previous reporting period of the combined entities on a pro forma basis. Disclosure in the pooling case includes the results of operations of the separate companies for the period prior to the consummation of the combination. In addition, pooling disclosure requires a reconciliation of those earnings previously reported and the restated earnings.

2. Failure to Give Adequate Information About Combined Entities Subsequent to Combination

Since analysts have as one of their objectives the determination of the components of earnings growth and the extent to which it is internally generated as opposed to being acquired, they also are interested in knowing the results of an acquired entity subsequent to its acquisition. The almost universal failure of corporations to supply these kinds of data is considered a serious deficiency. Analysts generally seek data about entities which have been acquired, both in the year of acquisition and in subsequent years. They argue that this information is essential both in order to evaluate the success of a merger program and to identify differential sources of growth.

This is a problem related to business combinations, although it is also a part of a more general problem of disclosure of the results of component parts by diversified companies which has been the subject of a comprehensive research study by R. K. Mautz under the sponsorship of the Financial

Executives Research Foundation.[1] The arguments presented in that study in terms of investor needs on the one hand and the difficulties of corporations in producing meaningful segment information on the other are relevant here.

At the same time the fact that a part of the consolidated group is the result of a business combination adds the significant dimension of acquired growth to the problems of evaluating the growth associated with many different product lines or business groups.

In one sense, it may be simpler for corporations to report on acquired entities than on segments of their operations which arose through internal growth since the fact that they did represent a complete business solves some of the problems of joint cost allocations. In our sample, 70% of the respondents indicated that the primary objective of the combination was to acquire a complete business to be operated as a largely separate and identifiable entity in the future. This would imply that reporting the results of an acquired entity would not represent a very onerous task.

At the same time, it must be recognized that once an acquired entity joins a consolidated group, it undergoes gradual but persistent change and hence its results will not long remain comparable with those it reported as an independent entity.

At the present time, however, it is quite evident that post merger results of acquired companies are virtually never disclosed. In the survey, no question was asked on disclosure of results of acquired companies in years subsequent to the year of acquisition; on the basis of a rather extensive informal review of reports, it seems safe to say that the number of companies making such disclosure is small. The survey respondents were asked about disclosure of the effect of the merger on sales and net income in the year it occurred, and the results summarized in Table 7 indicate considerable deficiencies.

The exposure draft stands mute on this subject, presumably relying on the Statement of the Accounting Principles Board and the SEC regulation on the subject of segment disclosure. These varying pronouncements will not deal solely with the problem of analysis of an acquiring corporation, however, and accordingly, it seems as though some improved disclosure of events subsequent to a combination might well be advocated.

---

[1] Mautz, R. K., *Financial Reporting by Diversified Companies*, Financial Executives Research Foundation, 1968.

Table 7   Disclosure of Impact of Merger

| | Combinations Accounted for as | | All Combinations |
	Pooling of Interests	Purchase	
Impact of combination on net income in year of acquisition disclosed ..	16.3%	6.7%	11.7%
Impact on earnings per share disclosed	9.4%	2.3%	5.9%

At a minimum, it would appear that disclosure of the contributions to earnings of acquired companies in the year of acquisition should be required. In those rare cases where no meaningful determination of acquired earnings can be made because business combinations represented simply the acquisition of operating assets which were integrated immediately into continuing operations, a statement to that effect should suffice.

Such a disclosure requirement will enable analysts to distinguish between internal growth which can be predicted to continue with a greater degree of certainty than can acquired growth.

3. *Failure to Describe Consideration*

The consideration given to the stockholders of the company joining the enterprise is commonly inadequately described. The market value of stock issued was rarely disclosed in the pooling situations in the survey. Of the combinations treated as purchase transactions, in only 28% was the purchase price disclosed. In addition, inadequate description has sometimes been given in connection with contingent payments which require the issuance of additional consideration at a later date.

The failure to disclose market value of shares issued in a pooling is of course related to the basic theory of pooling of interest accounting which provides that neither company acquires the other and hence the issue of consideration is not relevant. At the same time the comparison of market values would seem to have some significance even in pooling transactions since it would enable the reader to evaluate the financial commitment being made by the stockholders of the corporation issuing the stock.

In many cases, the reason for limited or non-disclosure was the reporting firm's judgment as to the materiality of the item involved. When a company undertakes numerous mergers in the course of a year, none of which are of a very large size, it is probably not practical in a published report to give details as to all of them. When one reviews the 100 page proxy statement including the financial statements of many diverse companies that are required by the SEC in some merger transactions one becomes aware that excessive disclosure can be a problem as well as inadequate disclosure. It would appear, however, that certain minimum criteria for disclosure should be established and met for all mergers.

The exposure draft does require disclosure of consideration in purchase accounting and disclosure of the number of shares issued in a pooling. It also requires that any contingent payments and other subsequent consideration be spelled out. It does not require that the market value of shares issued in a combination accounted for as a pooling be disclosed, presumably on the grounds of the pooling theory identified above.

4. *Description of Pro Forma Statements as "Historical"*

The practice of describing the combined statements of pooled companies prior to the date of pooling as historical representations of reality rather than as pro forma statements has been criticized. This practice is essentially related to the theory of pooling that the business combination does not create a new entity and hence combined statements of the past represent historical statements of the continuing enterprise. Since the companies were not in fact together historically it seems as though this application of the theory is somewhat dubious and that some caption other than the parenthetical "restated for poolings" should be given to differentiate historical results from retroactively combined ones. The exposure draft continues to provide for this type of disclosure in the case of poolings while combined historical summaries in the case of purchases are to be described as "pro forma." While this is not a major problem, it would seem that somewhat stronger terms such as "retroactively combined for comparative analysis" might be more appropriate for all combinations. This would emphasize that the previous year is presented to provide a base period with which to compare current performance rather than as an historical statement of operations during that period.

II. *Overstatement of Enterprise Results*

1. *"Instant" Earnings Through the Sale of Acquired Assets At Large Profit Over Historical Cost*

The abuse of business combination accounting that has probably received the greatest attention is the creation of earnings by a combining company through the sale of assets which had been on the books of the smaller of two combining firms at unrealistically low historical cost and the reflection of the profit on the disposition of these assets as profit of the pooled enterprise. The principal criticisms have occurred where it has been felt that for all practical purposes one company issued stock with a market value that reflected the valuation of the assets of the acquired company yet accounted only for the book values acquired through the use of pooling of interests accounting. A comparable problem arises when companies fail to properly record purchased assets at fair value and is discussed in the following section as inconsistent valuation of goodwill.

This is appropriately identified as an abuse in the sense that it represents reporting of profits that are not reasonably attributable to the time period in which they are reported. Hence the economic results for that time period are distorted and misleading conclusions may be drawn. The problem is mitigated somewhat if these profits require treatment as extraordinary gains. Only partially can this abuse be attributed to business combination accounting, however. It is certainly true that the accounting profession by adopting conventions of historical costs has created a situation in which profits are not placed in the proper time period when assets are held over a period of many years. This is particularly the case when a sale of significant assets takes place. The two questions that make the business combination problem particularly acute are the question of what entity reports the profit and the question of whether or not that is the entity which in economic reality it can be attributed to. If one group of shareholders of the combining shareholders agrees to issue shares in a quantity that recognizes appreciated asset value, it can be debated as to whether or not the realization of these increased asset values should flow through as earnings to the combined stockholder groups and hence show a rate of growth which when viewed in terms of the new reporting entity cannot be sustained. In a few cases to which attention has been called, common sense would say that economic realities are not being reflected.

Thus while these "instant earnings" can primarily be attributed to the accounting principle of historical cost, the principle of combination accounting applied also has an impact. Together they give rise to economic mis-statement particularly in the hands of managements who are keenly aware of the earnings impact of such asset sales.

The extent to which this abuse is present is difficult to tell from our empirical study since there is very likely to be a bias against disclosure of such items. The fact that a few of the most publicized cases of this phenomenon did not respond to our questionnaire leads to an additional subjective feeling that bias may exist in the results.

The survey indicated that 16% of the companies in the questionnaire sample sold acquired assets subsequent to the combination. The gain on the sale of assets acquired contributed on the average a 3% increase in net income reported in the first year subsequent to the acquisition. There was no significant difference in either the frequency of sale or the contribution to net income between combinations accounted for as purchases or poolings. The size of assets sold in relation to assets acquired, however, was twice as great in purchase transactions (20%) as in poolings (9%), which is the opposite effect than that which would be expected if many corporations were using this means of inflating earnings in pooling transactions.

Table 8   Incidence of Selling Acquired Assets Subsequent to Combination

	Poolings	*Purchases*	*Total*
Companies which sold acquired assets subsequent to combination	17.3%	15.6%	16.2%
Size of assets sold in relation to assets acquired (average)	8.6%	19.9%	13.1%
Percentage increase in combined earnings as a result of gain on sales	3.2%	2.7%	3.0%

The exposure draft moves to deal with these problems by a two-fold attack. First it identifies the intent to dispose of a significant part of assets as an event which will eliminate the possible use of pooling of interest accounting. In connection with purchase accounting, the opinion requires the revaluation of all assets to fair value on the date of acquisition except for the few situations in which the total fair value of the assets acquired exceeds the total consideration paid for the assets.

The exposure draft still permits pooled companies to record profits on the sale of assets that "would have been disposed of in the ordinary course of business of the separate company." Since many assets sales might well be so identified, the potential for instant earnings in pooling transactions still remains. In addition, this section places a two-year limit on the intention to dispose of assets and an agreement to dispose of an asset in two years and one day after the business combination may exist in a pooling transaction. Similarly, the practice of selling assets at a profit just prior to a combination and the recording of this profit as one of the joint enterprise through the pooling approach may still occur.

While it is clear that a substantial reduction of poolings as would occur under the exposure draft will reduce the availability of such "instant earnings" by revaluing the assets of one part of a constituent enterprise it will certainly not deal more comprehensively with the general problem of profit recognition on asset disposal where substantial appreciation in the value of the asset has taken place. In addition, "instant earnings" can also arise in purchase accounting when assets are not properly appraised and a part of the increased asset value is included in goodwill at the time of the combination. In the final analysis, this abuse can only be eliminated through periodic revaluation of assets for all companies and this path has problems as well as benefits.

2. Creation of "Instant Earnings" Through Post Year End or Late in the Year Poolings.

Another frequently cited abuse in business combination accounting is the practice of entering into pooling of interests transactions subsequent to the end of a reporting year or late in the reporting year and still reflecting the profits of the joined firms for the entire year being reported. The greatest dismay has been voiced in connection with poolings that occur subsequent to the end of the reporting year where under today's acceptable principles the entire year's result of the pooled companies are reflected in reported earnings. This has offended the common sense view of many users of financial statements that once operations of a period have been completed, the financial statements reporting on them should not be subsequently changed by an event that occurs following the reporting period.

There has been particular concern because of a feeling that, while a company's stock is still reflecting high multiples based upon erroneous expectations, some managements have gone out and found pooling partners after their own operations have failed to generate the kind of results which were expected by investors. These "high multiples" have been used to pool with other "lower multiple" companies based on relative market values and have thereby achieved the earnings per share objective antici- pated by the marketplace.

Our empirical results indicate that the distribution of pooling of interest accounting during the year is not heavily biased in terms of post year end or late in the year poolings. The survey results show 27% of the poolings occurred during the fourth fiscal quarter and 18% subsequent to year end but prior to the issuance of the annual report (of which three-fourths were retroactively included in the financial statements). No specific information is available for the effect of late in the year poolings, but post year end poolings which were retroactively included in the statements generally increased net income by less than 10% after excluding one pooling which increased net income by 50%. The effect on earnings per share was much smaller, of course, most frequently an increase or decrease of less than 2%. However, one pooling increased earnings per share by 13% and another resulted in a decrease of 9%. Although the averages are not large, the effect in any particular pooling can be quite substantial.

It is not entirely clear that this form of reporting does represent an abuse in the sense of mis-stating economic results if adequate disclosure exists. The accounting approach arises logically from the basic theory of pooling of interests accounting and from the accountant's view that the financial statements when presented should reflect the past meaningfully in terms of future expectations. If at the date of preparing a report, two firms have been pooled, the combined historical results of the entity are probably the most meaningful in anticipating future results. The accountant has felt that merely reflecting history as it existed on a particular day without giving adequate recognition to events occurring subsequent to that day would mislead rather than help users of financial information. It is only when one identifies the objectives of financial statements as measurement of past stewardship that questions can be raised with this approach.

The remaining problem of course is the basic one outlined above in discussing the possible confusion between historical financial statements and financial statements reflecting retroactively events that have occurred subsequently. With adequate disclosure of the results of the constituent parts of the organization a large part of the criticism of this form of earnings acquisition would disappear.

The exposure draft seems to deal adequately with the problem of disclosure, although by barring the inclusion of joined companies subsequent to year end it has tended to move toward the historical as opposed the future oriented interpretation of financial statements. This is probably justified on the grounds that it is consistent with the common sense canons of "fairness" held by an apparent majority of the users of financial information, even though it is not intuitively obvious why a combination on December 29 should be included for the full year while a combination on January 2 should not.

It would seem that if the Board had desired to deal with the problem in a consistent fashion it would either have accepted the current practice of retroactive restatement for post year end poolings with disclosure of the impact of the separate companies or it would have adopted an alternative approach of saying that basic financial statements should include only the results of enterprises under the direct control of the reporting entity and that activities prior to that point in time should be reported separately and combined only on a pro forma basis in a footnote. The former approach would show the pattern of operations on a consistent basis while the latter would represent an accurate historical reporting from a stockholder viewpoint. In this case the Board's compromise position appears to be a mixing of the two viewpoints which might confuse all by emphasizing an artificial time period rather than following a consistent theoretical approach.

3. *Artificial Growth Through Purchase Accounting*

It has been noted that net income growth can be made to appear very substantial as a result of purchasing a company even though internal operating growth is not taking place. When a company purchases another midway through a year, it includes the purchased earnings from the date of acquisition. If the acquired company is substantial, the combined net earnings in the year of acquisition will show an increase over the prior year due to its inclusion for part of the year. Then the earnings in the year following the acquisition will show considerable growth over the acquisition year due to the inclusion of the full year results of the acquired company compared to the partial year's results included in the former year.

The following results reported by a particular company illustrate this impact where the company made a major acquisition for cash midway through year 2.

Year	Reported Net Income		
	Company without Acquisition	Acquired Company	Company Combined
1	$1,557	$ -0-	$1,557
2	1,434	(7 mos.) 1,281	2,715
3	1,493	(12 mos.) 1,949	3,442

The portion of the acquired company's earnings included in the consolidation increased each year and accounted for a continued growth in combined reported net income even though the earnings of the acquiring company were basically flat during the three-year period and the total earnings of the acquired company actually decreased from year 2 to year 3.

Whether this is an abuse, of course, depends upon how it is viewed. On the one hand it can be concluded that legitimate growth took place from the viewpoint of the acquiring company's stockholders. Their resources were used to acquire the new subsidiary and clearly in Year 3 they owned the subsidiary for the entire year, whereas in Year 2 only a partial year inclusion was justified. On the other hand, it can be said in an operating sense that the consolidated income figure is misleading. Once again, therefore, the problem of the stockholder viewpoint versus an operating viewpoint must be faced.

A related question is whether or not purchased earnings growth is legitimate growth. This is a problem that neither analysts nor accountants have satisfactorily solved. On the one hand it seems clear that a number of companies have been consistently able to grow and benefit their own stockholders through acquisition programs. On the other hand, this is certainly growth of a different sort than the growth that occurs through expanding operations due to increased consumer demand for the products of the firm.

The exposure draft does not avoid this problem of artificial growth, although it does provide for improved disclosure of its impact through pro forma information for the full year of acquisition and the preceding year. Of course, the impact is ameliorated to the extent that the analyst also considers the related effect of the financing of the acquisition (e.g., additional debt or stock outstanding or reduced cash for use in the business).

4. *Artificial Earnings Per Share Increases Resulting from Differential Multiples Applied to Stocks in the Marketplace*

A frequently cited abuse attributed to business combinations accounting is the ability of a firm to show continued increases in earnings per share primarily through the vehicle of acquiring companies that sell for a lower multiple and thereby reflecting growth in earnings per share which is not real in economic terms. The following exhibit shows a highly simplified example of this impact. In this example Company A, by making an acquisition, was able to increase its earnings per share by 14%

although no increase occurred in the operating results of either of the constituent parts of the now combined enterprise.

Year	Company A			Company B			Combined	
	Net Income	E.P.S.	Market Price	Net Income	E.P.S.	Market Price	Net Income	E.P.S.
19x1	$1,000	$1.00	$40	$200	$2.00	$20		
19x2	1,000			200			$1,200	$1.14

Notes:
(a) Net Income is expressed in thousands
(b) Company A had 1,000,000 shares of stock outstanding before the acquisition
(c) At 1/1/x2, A acquires B for 50,000 shares of stock valued at $2,000 which is B's book and market value

This effect is not one that relates primarily to business combination accounting but rather to the highly divergent multiples placed upon earnings in the market place. Its identification as an abuse indicates the viewpoint held by some that analysts look excessively at earnings per share and thus do not reflect the fact that if the multiple differentials had economic merit the multiplier attached to the stock of the combined company should be appropriately reduced and thus no faulty market evaluation would occur. The accounting presentation will report the historical results from the stockholder's viewpoint but the dramatically different multiples applied to different stocks in the marketplace indicate that earnings per share is not the sole factor viewed but that significant qualitative judgements are made as well. There is no way in which accounting can eliminate the need for these qualitative judgements.

It has been sometimes indicated that pooling of interest accounting is in part to blame for the ability to produce artificial earnings per share increases. This depends upon the circumstances and the relative multiples of the stocks as well as the relationship between the acquired company's stock price and its book value. In the example above where market price and book value were approximately the same, pooling of interest accounting with restatement of past years would have indicated no growth in earnings per share while purchase accounting would show a 14% growth. In some cases, however, where the acquired company is selling at a price substantially in excess of its book value, pooling of interest accounting has contributed to the effect by making it possible for the acquiring company not to account for this premium. This effect is discussed below as another alleged abuse.

The exposure draft, of course, does not deal with the problem of diverse multipliers. This is essentially a reflection of the economic realities of the marketplace and must ultimately be coped with by users of financial statements in developing the evaluation models based upon reported earnings and future expectations.

5. *Artificial Earnings Per Share Increases Due to the Use of Hybrid Securities With Low Dividend Rates in Business Combinations*

An abuse that has been pointed out in prior years relates to the issuance of securities in business combinations which derive their value from the common stock of the acquiring company but which are styled as a senior security despite a low dividend or interest rate. When such securities were issued in a business combination in exchange for the common stock of an acquired company, no common shares outstanding would be added to the denominator of the earnings per share equation, while the additions to the numerator in income would far exceed the deductions in preferred dividend or interest payments. Thus an increase in earnings per share could be reported which was at least in part fictitious since the holders of the senior securities would have a call on common stock sufficient to significantly dilute reported earnings per share.

This abuse was substantially eliminated by APB Opinion No. 9 which required the disclosure of a fully diluted earnings per share figure as well as the inclusion of "residual securities" in the denominator of the earnings per share fraction. This was further refined in APB Opinion No. 15 on earnings per share which specifically included a carefully defined common stock equivalent in the primary earnings per share calculations as well as retaining the requirement for a fully diluted earnings per share figure. The exposure draft does not deal explicitly with this subject because the abuse has been remedied. It does leave, however, some situations in which earnings per share growth may be mis-stated in connection with business combinations as a result of contingency payment arrangements.

6. *Effective Date of Combination Set to Exclude Losses and Include Profits*

It is possible to time a business combination in such a manner that losses or periods of low earnings are shown in the period prior to combination and periods of high earnings are included in the first year of combination. Two cases of this have been suggested. The first occurs when a company with a seasonal pattern to its operations is acquired after the seasonal low point. Accounting under the purchase method would include only the high earnings óf the favorable season in the year of acquisition. Since earnings per share data is based on average shares outstanding, the earnings per share reported might not reflect a realistic trend in such cases.

A second more dramatic example is the case of companies which make substantial write-offs of inventories or provide substantial reserves for credit loss, obsolescence and so forth, under the guise of conservatism. Under purchase accounting, these losses may be recorded at any point prior to the acquisition date and thereby need not be reported at all by the combined corporation. Under pooling accounting, these loses would be recorded during the fiscal year prior to the year of combination and would thereby be shown as retroactive adjustments of the prior year by the combined company. In this pooling method, the losses would be included in earnings, but in the prior year, and would thereby improve the growth trend of the combined entity.

We sought empirical evidence of such phenomonon by asking for information about operations prior and subsequent to business combinations within a fiscal year but the response was so insignificant that no conclusions can be drawn.

The exposure draft makes no specific provision for the elimination of this abuse, although the disclosure requirements outlined above will have the impact of making it more readily apparent to the careful reader of financial statements. In the final analysis, the burden of protecting against this abuse must fall on the auditor and on the integrity of management.

7. The Creation of Large Amounts of Dubious Goodwill Through the Use of Dubious Market Values

An abuse of economic reality sometimes cited in connection with business combinations is the practice of companies with a thin market for their stock using the high price which this market might generate as a means of acquiring other companies and recording substantial additional capital and goodwill on the financial statements. Some companies with debt to equity ratios which might otherwise appear to be a cause for alarm have added to the paid in capital shown on their balance sheet by this device. Since this goodwill is largely the result of a high stock price created in a thin market, its economic soundness is subject to question.

The new exposure draft will not deal explicitly with this problem since it does call for the creation of goodwill through the use of purchase accounting. Some of the caveats in describing the basis for valuation of securities issued, however, may give pause to a few companies in reflecting the quantities of goodwill that have been shown in the past, as will the requirement for amortization against earnings. The fact that goodwill is being amortized, however, does not mend the abuse of recording excessive value on the balance sheet upon an inflated stock price at the particular date when an acquisition occurs.

8. *Large Elements of Cost Charged to Capital Surplus in Business Combinations*

A number of auditors and other insiders have noticed an increasing tendency in the past few years for corporations to charge substantial elements of expense associated with business combinations to the additional paid-in capital accounts at the time when the combination takes place. Many of these elements of cost are of the sort that would be called general and administrative expense in the normal corporation. The extent of this practice is extremely difficult to determine since these expenses are generally netted out in the published presentation of financial data. In our research questionnaire we made no specific inquiry as to the extent of costs charged to the capital accounts and accordingly, it is not possible to estimate the degree to which this is being done.

The degree to which this can be called an abuse is subject to dispute. It is a well established principle that the costs associated with the issuance of common shares should be netted against the proceeds rather than charged to expense and where stock is issued in a business combination, there seems no apparent reason to deviate from the principle. On the other hand, it is argued that in pooling of interests accounting, no new capital is created and there is, accordingly, no basis for charging expenses to capital accounts. Additionally, many of the expenses associated with a combination are argued to be costs combining the companies and hence have little to do with the issuance of stock. The new Accounting Principles Board Opinion effectively eliminates this practice. In so doing, it has opted for a solution without obvious theoretical merit presumably because of its feeling of the practical benefits involved. Without evidence as to the extent of the abuse, it is not possible to evaluate the costs and benefits of the Board's position. If substantial amounts of costs relating to the continuing administration of a company and hence properly chargeable to expense are involved, it may have the effect of making financial reporting more realistic even though it lacks theoretical purity. On the other hand, a more rigorous auditing approach to the elements of costs charged to capital might be a better answer.

9. *Overstatement of Return on Investment*

One criticism of pooling of interest accounting frequently suggested by analysts is that it dramatically overstates return on investment on a historical basis. When two companies merge on a pooling of interest basis the shares of the surviving corporate entity's stock that are issued are recorded only at the book value of the entity being combined. Where the market value of these shares is much higher it is suggested that the investment of the stockholders in the continuing entity is in fact much larger than that reflected on the books. The reflection of a high historical return on investment figured in such circumstances is misleading from a stockholder viewpoint since the stockholders of the larger corporation in fact gave up a much larger proportion of their market interest than was indicated by that which was recorded on the books.

This argument of course relates back to the argument mentioned above in the discussion of theory that the real cost of a business combination to the stockholders of the successor entity is not the book value but the market value of the shares issued. Some case can be made for this from the stockholder viewpoint even though in an operating sense it can be argued that where a going concern is acquired the operating characteristics are not dramatically changed by the combination. Where an operating asset with an unrealistically low cost is acquired for stock and accounted for as a pooling of interest, it is more apparent that an overstatement exists.

The new exposure draft will substantially eliminate this abuse since it will reflect most combinations as purchases.

10. *Non-Recording of Premium Paid to Acquire Company*

Another abuse attributed to current accounting practices for business combinations is the fact that acquirors are prepared to pay very substantial premiums for small enterprises both in terms of book and market values, at least in part because they do not have to record this premium if the acquisition is accounted for as a pooling.

It can be empirically determined that companies tend to pay a larger premium over market price for companies that are to be accounted for on a pooling basis than on a purchase basis. In our sample, for example, an average premium of 39% over the current stock market value of the acquired company was paid to acquire companies accounted for as pooling while the average premium in the case of purchased companies was less than 28%. There are various reasons why this premium might exist. Hidden or unrecorded assets might be more likely to be found in pooled companies. Tax considerations might be a factor although this effect would be likely to go in the other direction, since poolings more often qualify as tax free exchanges and generally do not allow the acquiror a new tax basis for assets acquired. Both these factors would tend to make pooling more favorable to the seller and less attractive to the buyer while the premium runs in the other direction.

Perhaps the most plausible explanation of this premium is that it may more easily be paid when it need not be recorded on the books. If some of this premium can be associated with pooling of interests accounting, it can be argued that companies are in fact paying something for an accounting method in excess of what the economics of the merger would otherwise justify.

The basic theoretical issues associated with this abuse however go back immediately to the question of how one views a business combination. If the basic concept of a pooling is accepted then no premium is in fact being paid because earning streams are merely being combined. Different degrees of interests in these earning streams are being determined by negotiation between the parties.

The exposure draft does mend this non-recording of premium paid by the substantial elimination of pooling of interest accounting. In purchase accounting the premium is accounted for. Whether it should be necessary to so account on the face of the balance sheet is of course a subject of debate. One possible alternative would be to disclose the amount of the market value of shares issued in a footnote to the financial statements without placing it on the balance sheet itself.

11. *Negative Goodwill Amortized to Income*

A number of people have cited as an abuse of business combination accounting the practice of amortizing into income an excess of fair value of assets acquired over price paid. While this does not occur very frequently there are some situations where assets can be acquired at a price less than their fair value in what is called a bargain purchase situation. The exposure draft will substantially eliminate this "abuse" by applying the difference between the price paid and the total fair value of assets acquired first to a reduction of the purchase price of long term assets.

Only if there is an excess of working capital over price paid will a "negative goodwill" figure appear. This will not have a substantial income effect since reduced asset amortization will have a similar effect to taking "negative goodwill" into income, but appearances will be improved. The theoretical arguments for the crediting of negative goodwill to income are not significantly different from those of amortizing positive goodwill. In one case the stockholder has paid more for fair value of assets and in the other he has paid less. In both cases from a stockholder viewpoint the amortization seems plausible while from an operating viewpoint questions arise.

12. *Contingent Consideration Not Properly Recorded*[1]

If a portion of the consideration to be paid in a combination is contingent on future events, it is not recorded until the outcome of the contingency is determinable beyond reasonable doubt. Thus a material part of the consideration given for an acquired company may not appear on the books for a period of several years subsequent to a combination.

In the case of combinations accounted for as poolings, the non-recording of contingent consideration is not a separate problem from the general one mentioned above. Under pooling philosophy, consideration has not been given, and the sharing of ownership interests is recorded in the increased number of shares outstanding with the related effect on earnings per share. Prior to APB Opinions 9 and 15, contingent issues were not reflected in shares outstanding for earnings per share computations and therefore went unaccounted for until the contingency was resolved. These opinions largely remedied this abuse, however. The first required the inclusion of dilutitive contingencies in the fully diluted earnings per share figure while the second included contingent shares in the primary calculation as well if the contingency was currently being fulfilled. The exposure draft eliminates this problem completely by making combinations ineligible for pooling of interests treatment where a contingency exists.

In cases of purchase accounting, the problems of accounting for contingent payments remain and are likely to grow more significant, since under the exposure draft rules, contingent payments are one device which can be used to make a non-accounted for payment in acquiring a com-

---

[1] The author is grateful to Thomas E. Huff, a Ph. D. candidate at Columbia University, for a number of the insights in this section.

pany.[1] Our survey indicated that 18% of the combinations in our sample involved contingent consideration.

The exposure draft does not change the current method of recording contingent consideration only when the outcome of the contingency is determined "beyond reasonable doubt", and the basic abuse of non-recording this element of consideration at the time of the combination remains. At a minimum, this means that there will be a delay in the recording of asset values and their amortization. Earnings during the interim will be overstated to the extent the asset amortization based on the full consideration paid for the assets will not be recorded.

Some contingencies based on security prices may represent substantial elements of consideration which will never be recorded. This is particularly true of contingencies which in effect guarantee a market price above that presently existing. Such arrangements are increasingly common in a bear market environment. For example, a company with stock selling at $10 a share might agree to issue 1 million shares in an acquisition with the proviso that if the price of the stock did not reach $20 a share within three years, the company would issue additional shares (or pay cash) to make up the difference. Such a purchase would be accounted for as a payment of $10 million and if the stock price did rise to $20, no additional consideration would be recorded. In such a case, it seems clear that more than $10 million was being paid in an economic sense, but the excess would not be accounted for either on the balance sheet or the income statement.

The exposure draft also draws a distinction between contingencies based upon earnings where additional consideration will be recorded and those based upon security prices where no additional cost will be reflected in those cases where the issuance of additional shares is a reflection of reduced market price. This implies that the securities contingency does not constitute an element of cost while the earnings contingency does. The logic of this distinction is not readily apparent. While an inconsistent rule can be applied mechanically, it is difficult to reason from and to apply to new situations which seem likely to occur in the contingency area. Contingencies based upon price/earnings ratios, certain commodity prices and some general price level index are just three of many possibilities.

---

[1] Under the opinions finally promulgated, this problem will be less acute since more combinations will qualify for pooling of interests accounting than would have if the size test had been maintained, and accordingly contingent payments will be used less frequently.

One possible answer that seems plausible is to value all consideration given, including contingencies, at the date of acquisition. This would create a substantial valuation problem but would reflect the economic cost most realistically. If valuation problems associated with contingencies are deemed to be too great, then ,a consistent approach based on value measured when the consistency is finally resolved might be used on the basis of objectivity with the recognition that economic cost is not being shown. The exposure draft seems to be lacking both on the grounds of consistency and in its portrayal of economic reality in this area.

III. *Accounting Inconsistencies*

1. *Pooling and Purchase Accounting Offered as Acceptable Accounting Alternatives to be Chosen at Will by Management in Many Circumstances*

One of the criticisms that have frequently been made of accounting for business combinations today is that under a number of circumstances managements may select the method of accounting they want as a simple accounting alternative. Under these circumstances it has been demonstrated that managements tend to opt for the alternative which maximizes reported net income which may or may not reflect the economic realities of the business combination. Under current practices, if a business combination is made for common stock or convertible preferred stock, management has the choice of accounting for the combination as a purchase or a pooling.

While some feel that there is nothing wrong with having alternative acceptable principles, the thrust of accounting in recent years has been to limit the extent to which this circumstance exists. Both accountants and analysts feel that widely divergent acceptable accounting principles are inappropriate unless they are used to describe essentially different economic facts. Under today's principles the same economic conditions may be described quite differently by the accounting principles chosen. While some say that disclosure will mend this problem, it appears that efforts should be made to avoid this circumstance. The exposure draft purports to eliminate the question of choice and, in fact, in Paragraph 42 explicitly denies the existence of choice. On the other hand. when one looks at the reality of the exposure draft it is clear the choice has merely been limited rather than eliminated completely. The requirements set forth by the draft for pooling of interests are so stringent that it is quite clear that an individual who might qualify could elect by some trivial adjustment in the terms of the transaction to not qualify and hence treat the transaction as a purchase. Thus if one were to summarize the effect of the exposure draft in this area, the choice of pooling accounting has been sharply curtailed but the choice of purchase accounting has been left open in virtually every circumstance. Nevertheless, by restricting pooling accounting, the Board has increased the comparability of treatment of business combinations. Those few companies that do qualify for pooling treatment, however, will stand out more dramatically.[1]

2. *Inconsistent Valuation of Goodwill*

Another inconsistency which appears on' financial statements is the method of measurement of goodwill. One set of measurement problems arises in the valuation of consideration given when it is other than cash. On a more practical basis, however, there is also an inconsistency. A large number of companies still record goodwill as the difference between the price paid and the book value of assets acquired, although the more conventional and generally accepted definition is the difference between price paid and the fair value of assets acquired.

Our survey indicated that slightly over one-half of the purchase transactions resulted in some portion of the purchase price being assigned to goodwill. Of these companies, 66% assigned the entire excess of the purchase price over the book value of tangible assets to goodwill and recorded no other intangible assets.

The exposure draft clearly identifies the valuation of goodwill as being based upon the difference between the price paid and the fair value of assets acquired. Also, companies are required to specifically recognize at appraisal values any intangible assets which can be identified and named. The significant cost of appraisal and the difficulty of measuring intangibles, however, make it likely that the problem of inconsistent valuation of goodwill will continue to exist.

3. *Inconsistent Amortization of Goodwill*

Under today's generally accepted accounting principles virtually any policy may be followed by a corporation in amortizing goodwill if goodwill is placed on the balance sheet. At one extreme corporations under the prescribed accounting for intangibles need not amortize goodwill at all. At the other goodwill may be written off over a relatively short

---

[1] Under the revised opinion finally issued by the Board, this problem will be more acute since the elimination of the size test makes pooling available in many more cases than would have been the case under the exposure draft.

period of years. The total write-off of goodwill to retained earnings is not an acceptable practice but it may be written off as a lump sum charge through income as an extraordinary item if in management's judgment it has lost its value. Thus management may adopt various accounting procedures for dealing with goodwill and clearly different managements following various procedures will come to significantly different results.

Accounting Trends and Techniques for the year 1967, for example, shows that out of 125 companies showing goodwill arising from acquisitions on their financial statements 48% were not amortizing, 24% were amortizing and 28% did not disclose what they were doing. Out of 177 companies showing goodwill in 1968, 54% were not amortizing, 17% were amortizing and 29% did not disclose what was being done. This would indicate a trend toward non-amortization but also very substantial variations in practice at the present time.

In the companies included in our sample, 56% were not amortizing the goodwill, 37% were amortizing (over an average of 16 years and ranging from 5 to 30 years) and 7% amortized the entire goodwill in the year of acquisition.

The current exposure draft will largely remedy this inconsistency for goodwill created subsequent to its effective date by requiring all companies to amortize goodwill over a period not to exceed 40 years. There will still be some variation to the extent that companies can justify a shorter period of amortization and methods other than straight line.

4. *Pooling Accounting Used Even When Shares Have Been or Are To Be Repurchased or Sold*

The final abuse that falls under the general heading of an accounting inconsistency is the practice of treating as poolings business combinations accomplished by the issuance of stock under buy back provisions or the issuance of recently acquired treasury stock. These devices are said to foil even the limited criteria which have been established as rules to distinguish between purchases and poolings by determining whether or not there is a continuity of ownership interest.

Where the continuity of ownership interest is only fictitious and its elimination is guaranteed by a buy back agreement, it seems doubtful whether the rationale for pooling accounting can be satisfactorily used. In the case of treasury stock purchase and issuance in a merger, the abuse is less clear. From a corporate viewpoint, cash has in fact been paid to acquire another entity since the treasury stock purchase and issue can be viewed as a wash transaction. On the other hand, from the viewpoint of the shareholders of the acquired company there is a continuity of ownership interest and pooling is therefore appropriate.

Our survey indicated no significant purchases of treasury stock during the year prior to the business combination. There were agreements to repurchase or redeem securities issued in 4% of the pooling combinations.

The exposure draft mends both these problems by eliminating both kinds of transactions from eligibility for pooling treatment.

A related problem is that of an agreement to dispose of shares received in a business combination. At the present time, current practice permits a merger agreement to provide for the disposition of up to 25% of the shares received in each of the two years following the combination while still maintaining eligibility for pooling treatment. Under the exposure draft, no limit is placed on the number of shares which may be disposed of by agreement after the combination as long as the acquiring company does not guarantee the purchase of the stock or the proceeds to be received. Thus an exchange can qualify for pooling treatment even if the seller has the right and the intention to register and immediately dispose of the shares he receives. This is justified on the theory that transactions among shareholders of a firm do not reflect the nature of transactions involving the firm. On the other hand, this approach does invite the practice of placing form over substance in the determination of proper accounting principles to be followed in a transaction.

Summary

In reviewing the various alleged abuses in business combination accounting, it has been determined that cases of inadequate disclosure, misstatement of economic reality and inconsistent accounting do exist under present generally accepted accounting principles for business combinations.

Some of these abuses can be attributed solely to the methods of accounting for combinations, but more are closely related also to much broader accounting problems such as valuation of assets and the nature of entity and thus cannot be fully remedied until the more basic problem is solved.

The extent of incidence of these abuses in the real world varies widely.

Some of the most publicized appear to be relatively infrequent happenings on the basis of our sample. Others occur very frequently since they are a regular part of today's established practices. Even when abuses occur infrequently, however, their impact upon the credibility of financial statements is out of proportion to the frequency of their occurrence and, therefore, steps to eliminate them are needed.

The exposure draft will remedy some but not all of the abuses. In some specific ways such as requirements for disclosure of post combination results of acquired companies and the adjustment of contingent issuance provisions, it needs strengthening.

On the other hand, some of the provisions of the opinion go beyond those needed to remedy abuses. The mandatory amortization of acquired goodwill, to take the most conspicuous example, does not seem to be required to protect the user of financial statements against economic misstatement and in fact its inclusion may create a new abuse of obscuring economic reality by confusing operating and stockholder oriented results.

Although many aspects of the exposure draft will significantly improve reporting for business combinations, it remains inadequate in some respects and excessive in others. It represents overkill if its primary objective is to remedy abuses.

V

EFFECT OF THE OPINION

CHANGES IN ACCOUNTING PRINCIPLES cause changes in financial statements which are generally easily predictable both in magnitude and direction. In the case of the exposure draft on business combinations, however, the effects are harder to predict intiutively because the change in acceptable principles may actually alter the nature of combinations.

It is therefore impossible to say with precision what the impact of the exposure draft will be if it becomes an APB opinion. At the same time, it does seem plausible to look at past business combinations for evidence that will help in predicting the effect of the exposure draft on the financial statements of combining companies in the future. This judgment is based on the assumption that most business combinations in the past were economically viable and useful transactions and accordingly would rarely be prevented by a change in accounting method, even though certain terms might be altered to some degree.

Several men interviewed by the author in the course of this study disagreed with this assumption. They believed an examination of past combinations to be irrelevant in predicting the effect of the opinion since many of the mergers which took place would not have occurred under the proposed principles or would have been negotiated on substantially different terms. They suggested a research plan based upon in depth interviews with a number of companies which had completed merger transactions with the purpose of determining what would have happened had the accounting principles outlined in the exposure draft been in effect.

This point of view and the suggested research plan were rejected. The basic premise of this argument is that the method of accounting for a transaction is a very major factor in negotiating the economic terms. Thus the method of measurement determines the economics of the transaction rather than reflecting its results. Since there is evidence that stock market prices do reflect reported accounting results,[1] even when identical economic entities report differently, it is reasonable to assume that some adjustment of merger terms will take place in the light of changed accounting requirements. The crucial point at issue then is whether the extent of this adjustment is so great as to negate predictions of the future based upon past transactions.

We were not optimistic that the suggested method of research would answer this question. Human beings find it very difficult to determine what they would have done in a situation if facts had been different. They often do not know why they did what they did let alone what they would have done. Thus interview data if it could be obtained would not be very reliable. Additionally, interviews would have had to probe the details of highly confidential negotiations from both sides of the transaction. The willingness of corporate executives to describe such negotiations in detail was subject to doubt. Finally, time constraints again were a problem.

We were also persuaded, perhaps as a matter of faith, that it was unlikely that accounting methodology was so important and so misleading that it produced a large number of mergers which were not justifiable on

---

[1] See, for example, Chapter VI

economic grounds. Our review of abuses did indicate that current accounting practice did obscure economic realities in some cases, but the evidence was that such situations were unusual. There is no support for the proposition that a significant proportion of mergers would have been unattractive without accounting aberrations. It also seems unlikely that the negotiating range available to parties in merger transactions is so great that very materially different terms would be arranged although legal specifics might differ significantly.

Accordingly, it was concluded that it was reasonable to predict the impact of the exposure draft by applying its provisions to past business combinations and observing its effect. We have done this for our sample of 1967 combinations, first by applying the draft specifically to combinations in the form in which they actually were accomplished and then by assuming that certain changes in the form of the transaction would have been made in the light of the revised requirements set forth by the exposure draft. In the latter case, we attempt to look at the substance of the merger transaction rather than at its detailed form, recognizing that a change in accounting principles of such magnitude will affect the specifics of the deal. By so doing the distortive effects of applying a new set of accounting rules to transactions which occurred under a different set of rules will be somewhat alleviated, and restatement of the past may provide an enlightening glimpse of the future.

The first step in applying the exposure draft to business combinations, therefore, was to determine the impact if it had been applied to the combinations as they actually occurred. Although this is a biased test because it does not allow for combinations which would have been differently structured to meet the more restrictive provisions of the exposure draft, it is instructive nevertheless to observe the impact of the exposure draft upon the types of business deals which flourished under more liberal accounting practices. Out of our sample of 191 business combinations (of which 98 were accounted for as poolings) only one would have met all provisions of the exposure draft and qualified as a pooling if the exposure draft had been in effect.

Table 9 indicates how many combinations in the three sample groups would have qualified as poolings under the exposure draft and how many would qualify under various alternative size criteria.

Companies which did not meet the criteria for pooling of interests accounting were then treated as purchases and goodwill was amortized on a 40 year straight line basis to determine the income effect of the

Table 9   Combinations which would qualify as poolings if Opinion is applied under varying size criteria

| | QUESTIONNAIRE SAMPLE | | COMBINATIONS IN WHICH ACQUIRED COMPANY WAS PUBLICLY HELD | | ALL COMBINATIONS IN SAMPLE | |
| | Group 1 | | Group 2 | | Group 3 | |
	All Poolings	All Combinations	All Poolings	All Combinations	All Poolings	All Combinations
3 to 1 Size Criterion (25% test) Total	98	191	90	118	162	276
# Which Qualify	1	1	7	7	8	8
% Which Qualify	1.0%	0.5%	7.8%	5.9%	4.9%	2.9%
4 to 1 Size Criterion (20% test) Total	98	191	90	118	162	276
# Which Qualify	2	2	8	8	10	10
% Which Qualify	2.0%	1.0%	8.9%	6.8%	6.2%	3.6%
9 to 1 Size Criterion (10% test) Total	98	191	90	118	162	276
# Which Qualify	10	10	15	15	20	20
% Which Qualify	10.2%	5.2%	16.7%	12.7%	12.3%	7.2%
19 to 1 Size Criterion (5% test) Total	98	191	90	118	162	276
# Which Qualify	15	15	18	18	29	29
% Which Qualify	15.3%	7.9%	20.0%	15.2%	17.9%	10.5%

changed accounting. In so doing, we measured goodwill as the difference between cost and fair value of assets in the few cases when that data was supplied, but in most cases we were forced to take the difference between cost and book value. This would tend to make income greater than it would be if some portion of this excess cost were allocated to assets since the asset cost would probably be amortized over a period of less than 40 years. This methodology does make the assumption that the price paid for the acquired company would not be adjusted in the event that purchase accounting was required.

The mean decrease in reported net income and earnings per share of the acquired company was 1.8% in the year subsequent to the acquisition. Since this is the impact of amortizing goodwill capitalized in only one combination by the acquiring company, the total impact of amortizing goodwill would be much greater upon those companies which frequently engage in business combinations. Table 10 reveals the impact of amortizing goodwill capitalized in combinations covered by our survey. The impact is of course greater in Group 2 (acquired companies which are publicly held) and Group 3 (the total sample) since these groups are biased in favor of larger acquisitions.

Table 10   **Percentage decrease in net income and earnings per share as a result of amortizing goodwill over 40 years**

		Group 1	Group 2	Group 3
			Mergers where Acquired Companies	
		Questionnaire Respondents	*Were Publicly Traded*	*Total Sample*
Decrease in net	mean	1.8%	8.9%	4.6%
income and	median	0.6%	3.9%	1.1%
earnings per share	range	0.0% - 28.6%	0.0% - 271.0%	0.0% - 271.0%

While these figurs are interesting, it is difficult to ascribe great predictive significance to them, because they are the result of applying the exposure draft to transactions which occurred in a different accounting environment. To make a more meaningful predictive assessment of the impact of the exposure draft, we must look at the economic substance of each transaction in order to decide what probably would have happened if the exposure draft had been in effect. Hopefully this will provide a proper basis for analyzing past combinations in the context of the proposed accounting principles. To do this, three assumptions were made:

1. When securities other than common stock were given in the combination, we assumed that common stock would have been given instead in order to meet the common stock provision of the opinion. To determine the number of shares which would have been issued we divided the market value of the consideration given by the market price of the common stock of the acquiring company at month end prior to the announcement date of the combination. By using a price prior to the announcement date we hoped to eliminate the effects of speculation or arbitrage. The assumption that common stock would have been given in all cases is biased, however, for there are many cases in which high yield securities are required to satisfy the shareholders of the acquired company. To the extent that such cases did exist which otherwise met the size criterion, our sample will show a higher number of poolings than would have actually occurred.

2. When treasury stock was issued in the combination, we assumed that newly issued common stock would have been given in its place.

3. When contingent payment provisions existed we assumed that they would have been eliminated in order to comply with the exposure draft. We made no adjustment for additional consideration which would have been given if the contingent payment provision had been eliminated.

Table 11 indicates how many combinations in our questionnaire sample (Group 1) would have qualified as poolings under these assumptions. In addition, various size criteria are tested. Table 12 indicates the combinations in which the acquired company was publicly held (Group 2) which would have qualified as poolings under our assumption, and Table 13 indicates those combinations in our entire sample (Group 3) which would have qualified. Although as Table 9 suggests very few combinations accounted for as poolings in 1967 would qualify as poolings under strict application of the new opinion, Tables 11, 12 and 13 suggest that a significantly greater number would qualify as poolings if it is assumed that the combination agreements would have been arranged differently to meet the provisions of the exposure draft. This indicates that while poolings would be substantially curtailed under the exposure draft criteria, they would not be eliminated completely.

Table 11 **Size Criterion Test for Sample of Questionnaire Respondents (Group 1)**

Size Relationship	Number of Companies Which Would Qualify as Pooling Companies who Accounted for Mergers as:			
	Pooling	Purchase	Part Purchase, Part Pooling	Total
Sample Size	98	90	3	191
3 to 1 (25%)	10 10.2%	0 –	0 –	10 5.2%
4 to 1 (20%)	11 11.2%	0 –	0 –	11 5.8%
9 to 1 (10%)	25 25.5%	2 2.2%	1 33.3%	28 14.7%
19 to 1 (5%)	35 35.7%	6 6.6%	2 66.7%	43 22.5%

Table 12 **Size Criterion Test for Sample of Publicly Held Companies (Group 2)**

Size Relationship	Number of Companies Which Would Qualify as Pooling Companies who Accounted for Mergers as:			
	Pooling	Purchase	Part Purchase, Part Pooling	Total
Sample Size	90	24	5	119
3 to 1 (25%)	33 36.6%	2 8.3%	0 –	35 29.4%
4 to 1 (20%)	38 42.2%	2 8.3%	0 –	40 33.6%
9 to 1 (10%)	60 66.7%	4 16.7%	1 20.0%	65 54.6%
19 to 1 (5%)	69 76.7%	5 20.8%	2 40.0%	76 63.9%

As expected, the 3 to 1 size criterion militates against pooling of interest accounting by large corporations. Of the ten combinations in our questionnaire sample listed in Table 11 which qualify as poolings, only three of the acquiring companies have total assets greater than the median total assets of the entire sample and only one has total assets greater than the mean. Further, it appears that imposition of any size criterion requiring the smaller entity to emerge with 5% or more of the stock of the combined enterprise to qualify for pooling accounting would effectively eliminate this accounting treatment in a majority of the business combinations which are now accounted for as poolings. Table 11 indicates that in our sample of questionnaires only 36% of combinations originally

Table 13   Size Criterion Test for Total Sample (Group 3) Including Cash Purchases

| Size Relationship | Number of Companies Which Would Qualify as Pooling Companies who Accounted for Mergers as: | | | |
	Pooling	Purchase	Part Purchase, Part Pooling	Total
Sample Size	162	108	6	276
3 to 1 (25%)	35 21.6%	9 8.3%	0 –	44 15.9%
4 to 1 (20%)	41 25.3%	14 13.0%	0 –	55 19.9%
9 to 1 (10%)	68 42.0%	22 20.4%	1 16.6%	91 33.0%
19 to 1 (5%)	86 53.1%	35 32.4%	2 33.3%	123 44.6%

accounted for as poolings would have met a 19 to 1 (5% stock ownership) size criterion even under our liberal assumptions. A more general idea of the restrictiveness of the size criterion can be gained from Table 13. This shows that in our total sample of 276 combinations, which is biased in favor of the larger combinations, only 45% would have met a 19 to 1 size criterion.[1]

The second area of the opinion whose impact was tested was mandatory amortization of goodwill. To determine the effect of amortizing

---

[1] Subsequent to this study, a survey of the impact of the size test on 1969 mergers was undertaken by Arthur Andersen & Co. using basic merger data gathered by W. T. Grimm & Co. This survey examined 1,452 cases where stock was offered in a business combination. Convertible preferred stock was translated into common stock for purposes of the size test. The results were as follows:

Size Test Ratio	Percentage of cases qualifying for pooling under size test
3 to 1	5%
6 to 1	11
9 to 1	17
12 to 1	23
15 to 1	28
19 to 1	33
24 to 1	39
33 to 1	46
49 to 1	55
99 to 1	71

The data used were not verified.

goodwill, we computed a goodwill factor for all combinations which did not qualify as pooling under the three assumptions above. The impact of amortization on all questionnaire respondents would be small in relation to total income. The mean impact of these combinations on net income of the combined enterprise was 1.2% and the range was from 0 to 12%. In the sample of larger mergers where the acquired entity was publicly traded, the impact was greater, averaging 8.6%. This mean was biased by an extreme case, however, and the median of 2.0% is a better indication of the usual effect. These data reveal the impact of amortizing goodwill created in only one business combination. The cumulative impact would be much greater for companies which make frequent acquisitions.

Another method of analyzing the impact of amortizing goodwill is to look at the effect of the amortization on net income of the acquired company subsequent to the acquisition. In those combinations which did not qualify as poolings in the questionnaire sample (Group 1) amortization of goodwill would have decreased earnings of the acquired company in the year subsequent to the acquisition by an average (mean) of 50.4%. The median decrease in earnings as a result of amortization is 26.3%. The effect of amortization in the first year is to destroy a large part of the incremental operating earnings brought in by the acquisition. The inclusion of such a material stockholder oriented charge may obscure the trend in operating performance being achieved by the acquired entity.

The final area of the exposure draft with which we will deal is that of bargain purchases. The exposure draft requires that when bargain purchase situations arise the amount of "negative goodwill"—the excess of fair value of assets acquired over price paid—be applied first as a charge against fixed assets acquired in the combination. There should be very few cases in which the amount of negative goodwill exceeds the fair value of fixed assets acquired. The result is that negative goodwill is taken into income implicitly through lower depreciation on fixed assets acquired in the merger. In our survey of 276 business combinations, 13 bargain purchase situations arose. One company amortized negative goodwill to retained earnings in the year of acquisition, one amortized it to income over three years, and one did not amortize. The remaining ten cases amortized negative goodwill to income in the year of acquisition. Applying the exposure draft to these combinations would have resulted in a mean decrease in fixed assets acquired of 30%.

Summary and Conclusions

Applying the exposure draft to prior business combinations has provided some interesting insights into what the structure of business combinations may be if the exposure draft is put into effect. Clearly some combinations in which a security other than common stock would previously have been given will take place for common stock if the exposure draft is in effect. On the other hand, the incentive for issuing common stock will be less great than before for those companies which fail to meet the 3 to 1 size criterion. Thus the total number of combinations in which common stock is given in exchange may actually decline.

The impact of goodwill amortization on corporate behavior is difficult to ascertain. Results of applying the exposure draft indicate that for many acquiring companies the effect of amortization will be severe and will tend to obscure the operating performance of the entity. Clearly the amortization will greatly reduce incremental earnings of the acquired company. It is possible that such a requirement will discourage the completion of combinations which have the potential of producing operating economies by not measuring that benefit fully in the net income which results.

Further tests of the impact of the exposure draft should be made. The analysis developed here is preliminary and of limited sophistication but the samples and test are sufficiently representative that insight into the impact of the exposure draft is gained.

VI

SURVEY OF ANALYSTS

SINCE WHATEVER FORM of business combination accounting that is ultimately chosen must be useful and understandable to users of financial statements, it seemed an appropriate part of this study to survey a group of the most sophisticated users of financial information both to get their opinion as to how combinations should be accounted for and to see if in their evaluation of securities they were influenced by accounting methods used.

The group we selected for sampling was the membership of the Institute of Chartered Financial Analysts. This group was picked as the most professionally qualified users of financial statements since their membership requirements include both experience in financial analysis and examinations which require among other things the demonstration of technical competence in understanding financial statements.

Credit analysts were not included in the sample since it was felt that their primary interest was in cash flows rather than income measurement, and for their purposes, business combination accounting seemed of less significance. Investment bankers also might have been surveyed, but it was felt that since many CFAs are with investment banking firms, this group had at least been sampled. It seems likely, however, that men who were primarily involved in putting companies together would have a somewhat different view than those whose primary purpose is the analyses of securities for investment. Time did not permit the specific investigation of this group.

Our survey was mailed to 1,200 CFAs, representing approximately one half the membership of the Institute. It was mailed on Columbia University stationery to avoid any possible bias resulting from the sponsorship of the project. We received responses from 211, or 17.6%. A copy of the questionnaire is included as Appendix B.

Analyst's Preferences

The first part of the questionnaire presented a merger of two companies accomplished by the issuance of common stock accounted for first as a pooling and then as a purchase with amortization of goodwill over 40 years. All factors other than accounting treatment were constant in the two cases. In both cases the data was presented simply, but the disclosure met the requirements of the exposure draft. The pooling case, therefore, restated results for the year prior to the merger while the purchase case did not but did disclose pro forma net income for the prior year. While the merger was fairly substantial, the impact of differential accounting treatment on earnings per share was only about 4%.

Analysts were asked which method of presentation presented the data in a more meaningful fashion from an analyst's viewpoint, and the reasons why they preferred that method. Since the case was a simplified one, the analysts were being asked primarily to indicate their preference for an accounting method in general rather than for an analysis in depth of a specific case. The results indicated an almost equal split in preference as indicated in Table 14.

Table 14   Analysts' Preference

	No.	*%*
Purchase preferred	98	46.7
Pooling preferred	91	43.3
No difference	21	10.0
	210	100.0

In giving reasons, those who preferred pooling accounting stressed its benefits in reflecting operations more meaningfully and a number mentioned the greater predicability of earnings under the method. The proponents of purchase accounting generally emphasized that it reflected stockholder investment more meaningfully and that it was more conservative.

Most of those who were most concerned and wrote extensive comments strongly opposed the exposure draft, although there was no unanimity in what aspects were most criticized. Some were particularly opposed to goodwill amortization—one called it "one of those self-flagellatory devices which is supposed to be good for one because it hurts"—while others complained about booking only part of a firm's goodwill, the use of stock prices to establish fair value and the existence of "instant earnings."

One thread that ran through several of the letters was concern that the Board was too committed to finding a single answer and not sufficiently intent upon adequate disclosure. There seemed to be a general feeling that someone determined to do so could follow the letter and ignore the spirit of any rules established. To quote one analyst:

"There is no way the APB can beat the likes of such a manager. He can find a loophole in anything except a catchall full and complete disclosure rule.

"The security analysts, the SEC and investment advisors have not been able to protect people from their own hopes and capacity for self delusion. Yet if the pertinent facts are fully disclosed—not just reported according to one of several formulae which can be chosen carefully—then the evaluation even of some risky companies shouldn't be so risky.

"This is a complex matter and one which defies a simple solution. I think the APB is using physical medicine for a disease which is largely psychological."

A similar sentiment from another analyst was expressed differently:

"Julius Caesar once said that 'men find it easy to believe what they wish to believe.' Corporate managements and the accounting profession have cooperated in some cases in the past few years to take advantage of this natural human failing.

"I believe that no formal techniques will ever prevent this process from going on if clear thinking and basic honesty are both absent. It seems to me that this is what should be demanded of management and of the accounting profession."

Amortization of Goodwill

A second question asked in the survey related to goodwill amortization. Analysts were asked whether goodwill should be amortized if it is recorded on the books of the acquiring company. Once again there was a fairly even split. In general, those who favored purchase accounting in the first question also favored amortization of goodwill while those who favored pooling did not. The correlation was far from perfect, however, as is indicated in the following table:

Table 15   Desirability of Amortizing Goodwill

	All respondents		Those who favored purchase accounting (%)	Those who favored pooling accounting (%)
	No.	%		
Goodwill should be amortized	110	55.0	79.2	29.8
Goodwill should not be amortized ..	90	45.0	20.8	70.2

Among those who favored amortizing goodwill, slightly more than half (54%) said that they would actually compute amortization for analytical purposes, while a very high percentage (91%) said that they would at least apply a lower multiple to earnings without amortization. Of those who opposed amortization, 61% said they would adjust earnings by adding back amortization (to exclude it) for purposes of analysis.

While most of the respondents were consistent in their treatment of goodwill amortization, the results indicate that a number at least felt that if no accounting entry was made, no adjustment should be made by the analyst to "correct" the accounting data. Those who commented on this said that they would make no adjustment because the market itself would make none in its evaluation of the securities of the company.

The Valuation Test

In addition to getting CFAs' opinions, it was decided to design a test to see if the method of accounting for a business combination did effect the valuation placed on a security by professional analysts.

The method chosen to do this was to develop a case in which a significant business combination was accounted for in three different ways: pooling of interests, purchase without amortization of goodwill, and purchase with 40 year amortization.

The analysts' sample was then randomly divided into three equal parts and each part received the case presented in a different way. Respondents were then asked to value the stock of the company at two points in time and to indicate a range within which they were quite certain (defined as 9 times out of 10) it would trade on those dates.

It was decided to build the case from a real company situation, although to disguise it so that an analyst would be unlikely to recognize the company unless he was intimately familiar with the industry.

The company selected was GCA Corporation, a medium sized company in the electronics field selling laboratory apparatus, instruments, contract research and specialized equipment. This company was chosen because it had a very material acquisition which doubled its size at the end of 1965 which it accounted for as a purchase without amortization of goodwill. This made the impact of different accounting methods material. The acquisition was financed by the sale of stock and some borrowing and the selling stockholder was paid off in cash.

Since the company did account for the acquisition as a purchase, it was easy to create this purchase without amortization and the purchase with amortization cases. It was somewhat more complicated to adjust the data to a pooling form since it was desired to keep the number of shares outstanding constant in each case. The repurchase of a number of treasury shares therefore had to be assumed and certain adjustments made accordingly in the capital accounts. After the data had been adjusted for the method of accounting, all raw figures were multiplied by 1.3 and the company's name was changed to General Precision Instrument Corp. for purposes of disguise. Per share data was not affected by this change since both financial figures and shares outstanding were increased proportionately. The impact of the accounting changes on earnings per share is shown in Table 16.

The case presented to the analysts included a two page text about the company which differed only in its description of the merger and complete income statements and balance sheets for the years 1964 - 1967. In the

Table 16   Impact of Accounting Method on G.C.A. Earnings Per Share

Method of Accounting	1965	1965 (Pro forma)	1966	1967
Purchase without amortization	$ .90	$ .98	$1.31	$1.47
Pooling of interests	1.02 (1)	(1)	1.36	1.53
Purchase with amortization	.90	.98 (2)	1.14	1.31

(1) Since pooling accounting provides for restatement of results in primary income statement, separate pro forma data was not required.

(2) Pro forma data does not include amortization. Impact of such amortization would be to reduce earnings by 18¢ per share.

text, market conditions were briefly described and the price earnings multiple currently being applied to the companies in the Standard & Poor 500 Index was presented at the dates when analysts were asked to value the company.

It must be recognized that a test such as this has many deficiencies as a simulator of actual behavior. In the first place, the respondents are aware that they are playing a game with the researcher and this has behavioral implications which cannot be precisely measured both in terms of time and effort devoted and in terms of the results reported. In addition, it is impossible to supply the analyst with as much information as he would in fact have available if he were actually making an investment decision. Many of the respondents complained that the information presented was not sufficient, and a number did not complete this part of the survey.

Nevertheless, the results of the survey do show that reported earnings figures are significant in the analyst's valuation process, at least so far as the process is replicated in this case. The respondents did not apply a significantly different multiplier to the earnings which had been reduced by amortization as compared to those which had not been so affected, and accordingly a higher market price was attributed to the company which did not amortize. Table 17 summarizes these results.

As a sidelight, it is interesting to note that analysts were not completely successful in putting themselves back into the 1966 and 1967 market environment in valuing G.C.A. The stock actually closed on September 30, 1966 at $23 and on September 30, 1967 at $69⅞. The rather significant difference may be taken as evidence of market irrationality,

Table 17   Analysts' Valuation of G.C.A. — Using Different Accounting Methods

	Number of Respond-ents	September 30, 1966			September 30, 1967		
		Median Price (1)	P/E Ratio	Range (2)	Median Price (1)	P/E Ratio	Range (2)
Purchase without amortization ..	63	25	19.1	18-33	30	20.4	25-44
Pooling of interests	74	26	19.1	20-32	30	19.6	25-45
Purchase with 40 year amortization ..	74	22	19.3	16-30	27	20.6	22-40

(1) Mean figures were slightly higher, but their relationships with each other were substantially the same as the medians

(2) Range data represents medians of analysts' estimate of range within which stock would trade.

of inadequate information made available to analysts, or of analytical deficiencies. Since the price of the stock, with no dramatic change in earnings pattern, has now returned to a below 20 level, perhaps the first of these explanations is the most persuasive.

Summary

The survey of a group of Chartered Financial Analysts, all sophisti-cated users of financial statements, clearly shows that their preference was almost evenly divided between accounting for a merger of two com-panies as a pooling and as a purchase with amortization of goodwill. In addition, the CFA's were fairly evenly divided on the question whether goodwill should be amortized; those who favored purchase accounting also favored amortization of goodwill and those who favored pooling did not.

Although there are many deficiencies inherent in the "valuation test", the CFAs did appear to be valuing entities using purchase account-ing and pooling somewhat differently. Pooling of interests was accorded a slightly lower price/earnings multiple than either purchase accounting with or without amortization. It does appear, however, that though pur-chase accounting was given a higher price/earnings for "quality earn-ings", nevertheless, the median price of purchase accounting with amorti-zation is lower reflecting the lower reported net income figure.

VII

SUMMARY AND CONCLUSIONS

AT THE CONCLUSION of an empirical study it would be comforting to report that the evidence pointed inexorably toward a particular conclusion which can be identified as the solution to the problem being studied. In this case it was inevitable that such a result not occur. At the beginning of the study it was apparent that no conclusion could be expected to emerge fullblown from the data and this would be the case even if substantial additional data were gathered.

The proper accounting for business combinations must inevitably remain a matter of opinion rather than of truth. What must be done, therefore, is to understand the practical results of the various accounting options that might be chosen and to determine subjectively which of these results is the most meaningful in terms of the objectives of financial reporting identified at the beginning of this study.

Empirical analysis presented herein does provide a number of insights which may be of value. In the first place it makes clear that the proposed opinion would have resulted in substantially different reported results if applied to 1967 mergers. These results would generally have been in the direction of reduced income and higher asset figures.

Second, virtually all 1967 mergers in the sample would have to be accounted for as purchases if all the criteria in the new opinion were applied to them. If it is assumed that what may be called technical provisions in the exposure draft could be met by changing merger terms in relatively minor ways, the major remaining constraint—the size criterion—would still have barred pooling by about 95% of the companies who responded to our questionnaires and about 90% of such companies that did use pooling accounting in 1967.

It was also demonstrated that the amortization of goodwill acquired in 1967 mergers over a 40 year period would only slightly reduce reported earnings in the years 1968 and 1969. At the same time, the impact of 40 year goodwill amortization on the incremental earnings produced by business combinations in the same companies would have been much more significant, averaging approximately 50% of the earnings acquired in the first year following the combination with considerable variation about the mean.

Even though the effect of goodwill amortization on aggregate reported earnings in 1967 was small, as many years of mergers are piled on top of one another, the amortization factor will come to have a material effect on the earnings of many corporations.

Finally, the various situations which have been labeled as abuses of good accounting practice either due to inadequate disclosure, misstatement of economic results or accounting inconsistency were examined to determine whether an abuse in fact existed and the frequency of occurrence. It was found that many of the abuses were primarily related to broader accounting problems than business combinations, although in some cases the fact of the combination emphasized the abuse. In a few cases, particularly in the area of disclosure, reporting deficiencies were found to be widespread. On the other hand, in the case of some of the most publicized problem areas, abuses were found to be relatively infrequent in number. At the same time, it must be recognized that such situations create attention and lack of investor confidence far out of proportion to their frequency and, accordingly, the research conclusion of infrequent occurrence is not grounds for inaction or complacency. A number of the abuses cited could be called such only on the basis of a subjective determination of what is reality, which is a reflection of the point of view of the perceiver.

In addition to these empirical studies, two other steps were taken. An examination of the accounting theory related to business combinations identified the distinction between operating and stockholder viewpoints as probably the most crucial issue in determining both theoretical and practical solutions to the problems. Most other issues revolve around the way in which this controversy is settled.

The survey of analysts undertaken in connection with this study proved conclusively that this group of users of financial statements is divided on what represents good accounting in this area. The group split almost equally when asked to choose between pooling of interests and purchase with amortization accounting both under the disclosure guidelines set forth in the exposure draft.

The second part of the survey did offer some evidence that the method of accounting used does affect the stock market value of the firm. Analysts' estimates of the value of the same company using different accounting methods reflected a significantly higher estimated price where pooling accounting was used as opposed to purchase with amortization of goodwill. This finding was additionally confirmed by the evidence that corporations were willing to pay more for companies when pooling accounting was available. The premiums offered over market were systematically higher in combinations where pooling of interest accounting was available than when purchase accounting was used.

These various findings indicate first that the exposure draft, if approved as an opinion, will make a significant difference in reported results and second that reported results are important in guiding economic actions. No empirical support was found for the proposition that the accounting really does not matter since it has no effect on economic realities. Accordingly, it is important that the Board reach a conclusion that is understood and supported by both users and preparers of financial statements.

In the light of this finding it is difficult to support an approach of permitting any accounting answer to business combination problems as long as disclosure is adequate. Even with comprehensive disclosure it is evident that users of financial statements respond to published earnings without appropriate recognition of their uncertainty and impreciseness. If the free market system is to serve its function as an efficient allocation of resources, therefore, it seems important that comparable standards of measurement be developed. Even if no "right" answer can be achieved, it seems that the weight of argument strongly favors the adoption of a uniform approach. Such a system, even if arbitrary, will achieve comparability and in time with an appropriate educational effort will come to be understood by users of financial information who will then be able to interpret the results as they see fit.

While it is recognized that the Board will have produced a prescribed rather than an inherently correct answer, it is important that this answer be one that eliminates accounting treatments which all agree have encouraged abuses and that it not obscure economic reality. While accounting is not equipped to accurately describe the economic realities of a business combination which is both a complex transaction and one involving a long time dimension, it should be able to produce information which will be helpful to users in perceiving the dimensions of reality.

VIII

ADDENDUM: A PERSONAL VIEW

IN A STUDY OF THIS SORT where many feasible solutions exist and no single one is demonstrably correct, it is almost impossible for a researcher to avoid developing his own ideas of the most feasible solution. These ideas are personal depending upon the researcher's view of the world and his weighing of various costs and benefits. The following conclusions presented therefore are solely those of the author based on his own value judgments.

The decision process which must be completed in arriving at an answer to the business combinations problem can be described as a sequence of questions. The first is whether current practice is acceptable as is. If this is the case, no further action is needed. However, there is general agreement that current practices are not satisfactory. The reasons for this are adequately developed in the section of this study on abuses.

The next possible solution is current practice bolstered by adequate disclosure rules. Since many of the cited abuses would not be remedied by this approach, the author believes that this is unsatisfactory. Some changes are desirable and they should include a prescription of what acceptable principles are in this area. While there is always the danger that a prescribed approach will force the description of diverse events into the same mold, there is a higher cost in terms of probable reporting deficiencies of leaving options open to management.

The next question is whether there should be only one way of accounting for all business combinations, or whether the circumstances surrounding each vary sufficiently to make them inherently different and justify different accounting prescriptions.

For both theoretical and pragmatic reasons I answer the first question yes, and here I depart from the Board's solution which recognizes alternative accounting procedures depending upon the circumstances surrounding the merger. My answer is somewhat qualified, however, to exclude from the category of business combinations a de facto reorganization of two entities where there is no apparent surviving entity and the ownership and creditor claims of the individual entities are substantially restructured. In such a circumstance, a new basis of accountability arises for all assets and claims and the books should be started afresh with current asset values recorded.

Except for the very limited number of such reorganizations, however, it seems to me that all business combinations are in fact similar in essence and the nature of consideration exchanged, relative size of the companies and other criteria do not change this essence.

A pragmatic reason for adopting this approach is the difficulty of establishing meaningful criteria which are not subject to misuse to differentiate between various classes of combinations. The exposure draft provides the classic example of this problem in paragraphs 44-47 where several thousand words are used to develop highly complex criteria which will be fully understood only by those seeking to find a way around them.[1]

Given this answer, the next question must be what method of accounting should be used. Here the pooling and purchase methods are the two available answers. If a purely operating view is taken of the business

---

[1] In the final opinion these paragraphs were simplified in a number of respects.

entity, the case for pooling is strong. If two operating entities are combined without any major change in their economic characteristics, the resultant entity could be viewed as simply the summation of the two parts. If accounting is to follow this reality, the combination should be accounted for by a similar process of summation which is the essence of the pooling approach.

While some bookkeeping problems may arise in applying pooling accounting to the case of a combination accomplished through the payment of cash, they are not insurmountable. Cash paid in excess of the book value of assets acquired represents essentially the retirement of equity similar to the purchase of treasury stock. While the cash of one entity is being used to retire the equity of another in a legal sense, under the pooling concept they can be considered as one. Thus a pooling accomplished with a cash payment would result in the simple consolidation of the two entities on the books followed by a reduction of the combined equity in the amount of the cash paid out. This would have the net effect of reducing the surviving corporation's equity by the difference between cash disbursed and the book value of assets added by the combination. This could be shown as treasury stock, as a new type of contra-equity account or as a reduction of retained earnings or paid-in capital.

Despite the appeal of pooling, it is not my choice. I cannot bring myself to abandon the stockholder approach which views the firm primarily from the owners' outlook rather than considering it simply as an operating entity. This approach is deeply ingrained in the assumptions of accounting theory, and the complete embracing of the operating approach required to select pooling accounting would represent a major departure from tradition in many ways. The implications of such a change would go beyond the purchase-pooling controversy and raise major questions about the all-inclusive net income concept which the Accounting Principles Board has been emphasizing. In a measurement scheme such as accounting which relies on familiarity and common sense, the lack of understanding which results from a change of this nature may have high costs to the users of financial statements.

If the operating approach is rejected as the sole basis for combination accounting, the purchase method seems to have stronger arguments on its side. A business combination is a significant economic event which involves the firm and not simply individual stockholders exchanging shares. The assets of the acquired firm undergo a majority change in ownership bargained by management and hence are no longer under the same economic control. This cannot be ignored as it is under the pooling concept. At the time of combination, the pre-combination stockholders of the acquiring company are in fact making an equity investment either through the use of liquid assets owned by them or by sharing their equity interest in their enterprise. From these perceptions I conclude that purchase accounting is a better reflection of reality than is pooling.

With this conclusion, the problem of how to account for the cost incurred in the acquisition must be solved. It is apparent that there is a significant difference between the purchase of a going business and the acquisition of a package of assets to be used in operations. In the latter case, cost need only be allocated to the identifiable assets while in the former part of the cost incurred will normally represent a payment for future earning power unrelated to specific assets. Total cost must presumably be determined by the fair market value of that given up be it assets or stock. In the case of stock, a number of the valuation problems discussed previously in the study must be solved although the quoted price of the acquiring company's stock is a reasonable starting point. An alternative approach with some appeal is to examine the buying company's analysis of what value it is acquiring in the combination and what it is paying in terms of its own expectations about its stock. This lacks objectivity but perhaps comes closer to a long term economic reality.

However cost is measured, the asset created by cost paid in excess of asset value is a fundamentally different asset than any of the other assets reflected on the financial statements since it is based on future earning power rather than being the cause of it.

The asset goodwill, therefore, should not be treated as an operating asset of the acquiring firm. It should be set forth in a separate section of the balance sheet as "Cost of Future Earning Power Acquired in Business Combination." Since this asset is the result of future earnings and not the cause of them, it is inappropriate to amortize the asset to the income statement. The basic matching model of accounting is based on the assumption that costs are incurred in order to produce revenues and thus should be matched against these revenues to determine income. Stockholder purchased goodwill, however, has no impact on the revenue stream of the firm. It is the operation of the purchased assets that creates the revenues. Amortization of goodwill as a charge against earnings would therefore distort operating realities and obscure the economic results of a firm's activities.

From a stockholder viewpoint, the capital invested in the earning power of the acquired entity is committed on a long term basis with no expectation of diminished value. If this value is reduced, it is not the result of goodwill being used up in operations, but rather from changing future expectations. Not only is such a change in value extremely difficult to measure since it is based on subjective expectations, but it is not a cost incurred in performing economic activities. The loss is the result of such activities rather than being an activity itself. Amortization will therefore not reflect use in any meaningful way even from a stockholder point of view.

While amortization of goodwill against income will make income a less meaningful measure of economic performance and hence should be avoided, at the same time it is apparent that there are practical problems associated with the perpetual growth of an asset of this nature over a period of many years. The amounts could grow so large as to overwhelm the operating assets of the business which would not represent a satisfactory common sense approach. The immediate extinguishment of the asset, on the other hand, would fail to reflect the economic realities of stockholder investments. The charging of amortization directly to retained earnings over an arbitrary period of time would do violence to APB Opinion 9 and the "All-inclusive income statement" rule which seems at the present time well ingrained in accounting thinking.

A possible solution to these various problems is the creation of a new stockholders' equity account. This account may be titled "Equity Representing Future Earning Power Acquired in Business Combinations" and should be created at the time when a business combination takes place. When new stock or warrants to purchase stock are issued in a combination, the amount attributed to future earning power should be set up in this section of equity. When cash or debt are given, the amount to be set up in this new equity account should be deducted from retained earnings.

The amounts in the asset and related equity accounts will then be gradually reduced over a period of years. Preferably, this reduction should be based on a percentage of the earnings of the acquired entity. If this is impractical, the reduction could be made on an arbitrary basis with full disclosure of the basis and the reasoning therefore. Disclosure of all other transactions affecting the accounts will also be required. In this fashion, as the earnings generated by the operations of the entity find their way into retained earnings, the equity account representing future earning power acquired in a purchase would gradually be depleted. While the problem of how to amortize goodwill has not been solved, its impact has been removed from the income statement where its potential for misleading is greatest.

This approach will have the benefit of reflecting a substantial stockholder investment involved in the acquisition of future earning power while at the same time not distorting operations. Operating results will be reflected in net income. The disclosure requirements for purchase accounting set forth in the exposure draft should be maintained and to this should be added the requirement that where the acquired company is maintained as an independent entity, its operating results during the year of acquisition and for one subsequent year should be disclosed.

An approach such as the one suggested cannot be defended on the grounds of absolute truth or even revelation. It does, however, meet most of the abuses identified as currently existing in the business combination area, it does reflect stockholder investment and it does not distort net income by the inclusion of charges not relevant to its determination. It maintains the basic stockholder orientation which has been the basis of accounting theory while at the same time producing meaningful operating figures. It also does not permit accumulation of massive amounts of goodwill which might mislead investors and others by obscuring the operating characteristics of the firm and it specifically identifies the asset goodwill by a description of its nature. It has the disadvantage of creating a new section of equity with the usual difficulties of education and understanding, and of reducing the historical meaning of the retained earnings account in the case of cash acquisitions of entities with material goodwill. If advantages are felt to outweigh disadvantages, it may represent a meaningful compromise between two currently polarized viewpoints.

APPENDIX A

BUSINESS COMBINATIONS RESEARCH DATA SHEET

ACQUIRING COMPANY _____ __ __ __ __   1–4/

ACQUIRED COMPANY _____ __ __   5–6/

I. General data about merger

    1. On approximately what date did negotiations begin?
                                                        __ __ __ __ __ __   7–12/
                                                       Month Day Year

    2. On what date was first public announcement made that merger was being contemplated?
                                                        __ __ __ __ __ __   13–18/
                                                        Month Day Year

    3. On what date were the terms of the merger announced?
                                                        __ __ __ __ __ __   19–24/
                                                        Month Day Year

    4. What was the effective date of the merger (actual exchange of assets or stock)?
                                                        __ __ __ __ __ __   25–30/
                                                        Month Day Year

    5. What was the primary objective of the merger (check one)

      31/   ___   1. Diversification: acquisition of complete business (not related directly to present business) to be operated as largely separate and identifiable entity in future

           ___   2. Acquisition of complete business (related directly to present business) to be operated as a largely separate and identifiable entity in future

           ___   3. Acquisition of assets, products or talents to be integrated with current operations

           ___   4. Other (please specify): _____

    6. If you checked answer 3 to question 5 above, please rank the assets, products or talents in order of importance (start with 1 as the most important; do not rank those items which were not important in the merger)

      32/   ___   New markets for current products
      33/   ___   Marketing personnel and organization
      34/   ___   New products to market through current organization
      35/   ___   Entry into a new product market
      36/   ___   Research capability
      37/   ___   Productive capacity (plant & equipment)
      38/   ___   General management talent
      39/   ___   Financial resources
      40/   ___   Other (please specify)_____

    7. At the time of the acquisition, was the acquiring company's stock:
      41/   ___   1. listed on New York Stock Exchange
           ___   2. listed on American Stock Exchange
           ___   3. traded over the counter or on a regional exchange
           ___   4. not publicly traded

    8. At the time of the acquisition, was the acquired company's stock:
      42/   ___   1. listed on New York Stock Exchange
           ___   2. listed on American Stock Exchange
           ___   3. traded over the counter or on a regional exchange
           ___   4. not publicly traded

    9. Date of acquiring company's fiscal year end
                                                             __ __ __ __   43–46/
                                                             Month Day

    10. Date of acquired company's fiscal year end
                                                              __ __ __ __   47–50/
                                                             Month Day

11. Please list any business combinations in which you were involved during calendar 1967 for which you did not receive a Research Data Sheet.

Acquired Company or Division	Price Paid	Net Assets Acquired at date of acquisition	Net Income Acquired(*)
	$	$	$

(*) Net income of acquired entity for nearest measurable 12 month period prior to merger

12. Please supply the following data concerning the number of mergers and acquisitions in which you were involved in the four calendar years 1966-69 and how they were accounted for.

	1966	1967	1968	1969	
Total number of mergers and acquisitions	— —	— —	— —	— —	51–58/
Number accounted for as a					
Pooling	— —	— —	— —	— —	59–66/
Purchase	— —	— —	— —	— —	67–74/
Part Purchase, Part Pooling	— —	— —	— —	— —	7–14/

II. Nature of exchange

1. What was the medium (or several media) used in the exchange and what was the market value on the date the exchange took place? For each classification of securities used, please indicate the basis of determination of market value by entering the appropriate index number in accordance with the following schedule:

Index No.	Basis for valuation
1.	Quoted market value on date of exchange
2.	Market value discounted due to restrictions on shares issued
3.	Market value discounted to give effect to cost of floating public issue
4.	Imputed market value (due to lack of public trading)
5.	Fair market value of underlying assets acquired
6.	Other (please specify)_____

a. Newly issued common stock
Number of shares	(001)	— —,— — —,— — — —
Market value of shares	(002) $	— —,— — —,— — —,— —
Basis for valuation	(003)	Index Number —

b. Treasury stock (common) acquired within one year of merger
Number of shares	(004)	— —,— — —,— — — —
Market value of shares	(005) $	— —,— — —,— — —,— —
Basis for valuation	(006)	Index Number —

c. Treasury stock (common) acquired prior to one year from date of merger
Number of shares	(007)	—,— — —,— — — —
Market value of shares	(008) $	— —,— — —,— — —,— —
Basis for valuation	(009)	Index Number —

d. Convertible preferred stock
    Number of shares of preferred   (010)   __ __,__ __ __,__ __ __
    Number of common shares into which preferred
      could be converted   (011)   __ __,__ __ __,__ __ __
    Market value of preferred shares (at date
      of exchange if available; on first day of
      trading if no quoted market value
      previously existed)   (012) $__ __ __,__ __ __,__ __ __
    Basis for valuation   (013)   Index Number __

e. Convertible debt
    Principal amount issued   (014) $__ __ __,__ __ __,__ __ __
    Number of common shares into which
      debt could be converted   (015)   __ __,__ __ __,__ __ __
    Market value of convertible debt issued   (016) $__ __ __,__ __ __,__ __ __
    Basis for valuation   (017)   Index Number __

f. Debt with warrants
    Principal amount issued   (018) $__ __ __,__ __ __,__ __ __
    Number of common shares potentially
      issuable under warrants   (019)   __ __,__ __ __,__ __ __
    Exercise price of warrants   (020)   __ __.__ __
    Basis for valuation   (021)   Index Number __

g. Other preferred stock
    Number of shares issued   (022)   __ __,__ __ __,__ __ __
    Market value of preferred shares issued   (023) $__ __ __,__ __ __,__ __ __
    Basis for valuation   (024)   Index Number __

h. Other debt
    Principal amount issued   (025) $__ __ __,__ __ __,__ __ __
    Market value of debt issued   (026) $__ __ __,__ __ __,__ __ __
    Basis for valuation   (027)   Index Number __

i. Warrants and options
    Number of warrants and options issued to
      stockholders other than officers and
      employees   (028)   __ __,__ __ __,__ __ __
    Number of warrants and options issued to
      officers and employees   (029)   __ __,__ __ __,__ __ __
    Market value of warrants and options   (030) $__ __ __,__ __ __,__ __ __
    Exercise price of warrants and options issued   (031)   __ __.__ __
    Basis for valuation   (032)   Index Number __

j. Cash — amount paid   (033) $__ __ __,__ __ __,__ __ __

2. Were there any agreements to repurchase or redeem securities issued in the merger transaction?

15/   __   1. Yes.
       __   2. No.

If so, what was the approximate percentage of the securities which were subject to repurchase or redemption?   __ __%   16–17/

What was the approximate period (in months) over which the securities could be repurchased or redeemed?   __ __   18–19/
                            Months

3. Were there any restrictions on securities issued? (check all that apply)
20/   __   1. Held under investment letter subject to S.E.C. registration
       __   2. Other limitation on sale
       __   3. Voting power restricted by voting trust or some other means
       __   4. In escrow pending satisfaction of various covenants
       __   5. Other restrictions (please specify) _____

4. Was there any provision for contingent payments based upon future performance?

21/   ___   1. Yes

       ___   2. No

5. If a contingent payment provision existed, what was the basis for determining the amount of the payment (check one)

22/   ___   1. Percentage of total subsequent earnings

       ___   2. Subsequent earnings over a specified level

       ___   3. Subsequent price of acquiring company's stock

       ___   4. Subsequent earnings and stock price

       ___   5. Other (please specify) _____

_____

6. What was the period (in months) over which the contingent payment was determined? __ __   23–24/
                                                                                 months

7. What was the means used in making the contingent payment? (check all that apply)

25/   ___   1. Cash

       ___   2. common stock

       ___   3. convertible preferred stock

       ___   4. debt

       ___   5. preferred stock

       ___   6. cash or common stock at seller's option

       ___   7. other (please specify) _____

_____

8. Was any stock of the acquired company owned by the acquiring company prior to the acquisition?

26/   ___   1. Yes

       ___   2. No

If so, what percentage of outstanding shares was owned?

27–28/   __ __% on date merger was publicly announced

29–30/   __ __% two years prior to merger

31–32/   __ __% five years prior to merger

9. How was the merger transaction treated for tax purposes?

33/   ___   1. Taxable exchange

       ___   2. Non taxable exchange

10. What was the book value (on the seller's books) of the various classes of assets and liabilities acquired?

Current assets	(034)	$__ __,__ __,__ __
Current liabilities	(035)	$__ __,__ __,__ __
Fixed assets (net)	(036)	$__ __,__ __,__ __
Long term equity investment in other companies	(037)	$__ __,__ __,__ __
Other assets	(038)	$__ __,__ __,__ __
Other liabilities	(039)	$__ __,__ __,__ __
Stockholders' equity	(040)	$__ __,__ __,__ __

11. What was the estimated market value of these assets and liabilities at the date of the acquisition?

Current assets	(041)	$__ __,__ __,__ __
Current liabilities	(042)	$__ __,__ __,__ __
Fixed assets (net)	(043)	$__ __,__ __,__ __
Long term equity investment in other companies	(044)	$__ __,__ __,__ __
Other assets	(045)	$__ __,__ __,__ __
Other liabilities	(046)	$__ __,__ __,__ __
Stockholders' equity	(047)	$__ __,__ __,__ __

12. Where market value exceeded book values of assets acquired, please indicate (in months) the average period of time over which these assets would be estimated to be held before sale or disposition

Inventories	— — months	34–35/
Fixed assets	— — months	36–37/
Investments	— — months	38–39/
Other assets	— — months	40–41/

13. Please supply the following data about the capital structure of the buying company immediately prior to the exchange:

Common shares outstanding	(048)	— — —,— — —,— — —
Common stockholders' equity	(049)	$— —,— — —,— — —,— — —
Shares issuable on conversion of preferred stock or debt	(050)	— —,— — —,— — —
Shares issuable on exercise of warrants and options	(051)	— —,— — —,— — —

III. Accounting for exchange

1. How was exchange accounted for on the books?

42/
- — 1. Pooling of interest
- — 2. Purchase
- — 3. Part purchase, part pooling
- — 4. Other (please specify) _____

2. If purchase accounting was used and consideration given differed from book value of net assets acquired, how was this difference accounted for?

(052) $— — —,— — —,— — — assigned to tangible assets
(053) $— — —,— — —,— — — assigned to intangible assets other than goodwill
(054) $— — —,— — —,— — — assigned to goodwill

3. If goodwill was created, how was it accounted for? (check one)

43/
- — 1. Not amortized
- — 2. Amortized immediately to retained earnings
- — 3. Amortized to income as extraordinary item in year of acquisition
- — 4. Amortized to income (not extraordinary) in year of acquisition
- — 5. Amortized over time
- — 6. Other (please specify) _____

4. If goodwill was amortized over time, what was the time period (in years)? — — years 44–45/

5. What was the basis for amortization over this time period? (check one)

46/
- — 1. Straight line
- — 2. Based on some percentage of earnings
- — 3. Systematic accelerated method (such as sum of the years digits)
- — 4. Other (please specify) _____

6. How much amortization was included in expense?

a. In year of acquisition	(055)	$— — —,— — —,— — —
b. In first fiscal year subsequent to acquisition	(056)	$— — —,— — —,— — —
c. In second fiscal year subsequent to acquisition	(057)	$— — —,— — —,— — —

7. Did acquisition take place subsequent to the end of the fiscal year but prior to the issuance of the annual report?

47/
- — 1. Yes
- — 2. No

a. If so, were the operating results of the acquired company included in the financial statements presented for the fiscal year in the annual report? (This means in the financial statements, not simply in footnotes)

48/ ___ 1. Yes
___ 2. No

b. If so, was the impact of the acquired company on the year's financial statements explicitly disclosed (check all that apply)

49/ ___ 1. Yes, in the face of the statement
___ 2. Yes, in footnotes
___ 3. Yes, but not in the statements or notes
___ 4. No

c. What was the percentage impact of the acquired company?

a. On net income ___ ___ ___% 50–52/

b. On earnings per share ___ ___ ___% 53–55/

(percentages should be computed by relating the change in income and earnings per share to the total reported figures including the merger company; please indicate decreases by parentheses).

8. If pooling of interests accounting was used, were prior years restated to give effects to the pooling on a retroactive basis?

56/ ___ 1. Yes
___ 2. No, since effect was immaterial
___ 3. No, since no prior year data was furnished in the annual report
___ 4. No

9. If purchase accounting was used, what financial data relating to the acquired company prior to the merger was disclosed in the acquiring company's annual report? (Check any applicable item)

57/ ___ 1. None
___ 2. Net income and sales data for any portion of acquiring company's fiscal year prior to merger
___ 3. Net income and sales data for the year prior to the year of the merger
___ 4. Other (please specify) _____

_____

10. Have you sold any fixed assets or investments of the acquired company subsequent to the acquisition?

58/ ___ 1. Yes
___ 2. No

A. If so, what was
a. The book value of these assets (058) $___ ___,___ ___,___ ___ ___
b. The selling price of the assets (059) $___ ___,___ ___,___ ___ ___

B. If so, how did you account for profit (or loss) on sale? (Check any applicable item)

59/ ___ 1. Part of operating income
___ 2. Non operating or non-recurring items before extraordinary items
___ 3. Extraordinary items

11. Has there been a significant reduction in inventory acquired in the combination?

60/ ___ 1. Yes
___ 2. No.

A. If so, was inventory costed on a LIFO basis?

61/ ___ 1. Yes
___ 2. No

B. What was the amount of gain or loss included
in income attributable to this disposition? (060)$___ __ __,__ __ __,__ __ __

C. Was it separately identified on the income statement?
62/ ___ 1. Yes
___ 2. No

IV. Nature of disclosure made in published reports

1. Did you disclose in an interim report that the merger had taken place?
63/ ___ 1. Yes
___ 2. No

In your annual report?
64/ ___ 1. Yes
___ 2. No

(Note: This means was explicit mention made, including company name)

2. Did you disclose the fair market value of all consideration given in published reports?
65/ ___ 1. Yes
___ 2. No

3. Did you explicitly disclose the impact of the merger:
a. on net income in the current year?
66/ ___ 1. Yes
___ 2. No

b. on earnings per share in the current year
67/ ___ 1. Yes
___ 2. No

4. If you did not disclose the impact explicitly, did you give sufficient information so the
impact could be computed by an analyst?
68/ ___ 1. Yes
___ 2. No

5. If prior year statements were restated, did you disclose the impact of merged companies
on the restated prior year statements?
69/ ___ 1. Yes
___ 2. No

6. If prior year statements were not restated, did you give sufficient information so that an
analyst could reconstruct prior years net income on a pro forma basis if he wished to?
70/ ___ 1. Yes
___ 2. No

7. Did either company in the merger have a tax loss carryover?
a. buying company
71/ ___ 1. Yes
___ 2. No

b. acquired company
72/ ___ 1. Yes
___ 2. No

c. If so, was amount of carryover disclosed in annual report?
73/ ___ 1. Yes
___ 2. No

V. Financial Data

In this section, data is requested relating both to the acquiring and acquired companies, both before and after the merger. It is recognized that data with regard to the acquired company subsequent to the merger may be difficult to determine if the company is not maintained as a separate entity. Even if it is maintained separately it is clear that overhead charges, cost saving effects, transfer pricing and other changes may make the data less than fully comparable with pre-merger data. Nevertheless, since post-merger data are very important in drawing conclusions about the usefulness of varying accounting methods, we would appreciate your best estimates.

1. Please supply the following data for the buying company as it was originally reported in the annual reports for the years requested.

	For fiscal year ending			For fiscal year ending			For fiscal year ending		
	(061) Month	Day	6 4 Year	(062) Month	Day	6 5 Year	(063) Month	Day	6 6 Year
Income Statement Items									
Sales	(068)$			(069)$			(070)$		
Net income before extraordinary items	(075) $			(076) $			(077) $		
Extraordinary items	(082) $			(083) $			(084) $		
Earnings per share	(089) $			(090) $			(091) $		
Fully diluted earnings per share (per APB Opinion 15)	(096) $			(097) $			(098) $		
Balance Sheet Items									
Total assets	(103)$			(104)$			(105)$		
Goodwill	(110) $			(111) $			(112) $		
Stockholders' equity	(117)$			(118)$			(119)$		
Common shares outstanding	(124)			(125)			(126)		
Additional common shares issuable on conversion of securities and exercise of warrants and options	(131)			(132)			(133)		

2. Adjusted financial data: the purpose of this section is to assemble data for the buying company which is comparable over time. Adjustments for three groups of data are requested:

(a) Three years prior to acquisition: Please supply these data as restated in the annual report of the buying company for the fiscal year in which the merger took place. If no restatements were made these three columns may be left blank.

	(a) 3 years prior to acquisition as restated in year of merger								
	Fiscal year ending			Fiscal year ending			Fiscal year ending		
	(138) Month	Day	Year	(139) Month	Day	Year	(140) Month	Day	Year
Income Statement Items									
Sales	(144)$			(145)$			(146)$		
Net income before extraordinary items	(150) $			(151) $			(152) $		
Extraordinary items	(156) $			(157) $			(158) $		
*Earnings per share	(162) $			(163) $			(164) $		
*Fully-diluted earnings per share (per APB Opinion 15)	(168) $			(169) $			(170) $		
Balance Sheet Items									
Total assets	(174)$			(175)$			(176)$		
Goodwill	(180) $			(181) $			(182) $		
Stockholders' equity	(186)$			(187)$			(188)$		
*Common shares outstanding	(192)			(193)			(194)		

* Please compute earnings per share data for section (a) on basis of restated data as presented in annual report for the year of the merger. For section (b), the computation should show what earnings per share would have been were it not for mergers during the year, thus excluding both earnings and additional shares resulting from mergers. For section (c), the computation should include

Where the acquired company is not maintained as a separate entity, we would like you to estimate sales and profits attributable to the business acquired. Where it is separate, book data will be satisfactory unless there is some clear reason why it does not represent a fair measure of post-merger perfomance.

Please determine extraordinary items in accordance with Opinion 9 of the Accounting Principles Board. Thus extraordinary items may include items which you charged to retained earnings or included in operating income prior to the issuance of the Opinion. In all cases please denote negative values by parentheses.

If you feel that it will be helpful to include explanatory comments, please attach them on a separate sheet.

	For fiscal year ending				For fiscal year ending				For fiscal year ending				For fiscal year ending		
(064)			**6 7**	(065)			**6 8**	(066)			**6 9**	(067)			**7 0**
	Month	Day	Year		Month	Day	Year		Month	Day	Year		Month	Day	Year
(071)$				(072)$				(073)$				(074)$			
(078) $				(079) $				(080) $				(081) $			
(085) $				(086) $				(087) $				(088) $			
(092) $				(093) $				(094) $				(095) $			
(099) $				(100) $				(101) $				(102) $			
(106)$				(107)$				(108)$				(109)$			
(113) $				(114) $				(115) $				(116) $			
(120)$				(121)$				(122)$				(123)$			
(127)				(128)				(129)				(130)			
(134)				(135)				(136)				(137)			

(b) Year of the acquisition: Please supply the data requested for the buying company as they would have appeared if the acquisition had not taken place.

(c) Two fiscal years subsequent to the acquisition: Please adjust these figures by excluding acquisitions which occurred in 1968 or 1969.

(b) Year of acquisition without effect of merger			(c) Two fiscal years subsequent to acquisition					
Fiscal year ending			Fiscal year ending			Fiscal year ending		
(141)			(142)			(143)		
Month	Day	Year	Month	Day	Year	Month	Day	Year
(147)$			(148)$			(149)$		
(153) $			(154) $			(155) $		
(159) $			(160) $			(161) $		
(165) $			(166) $			(167) $		
(171) $			(172) $			(173) $		
(177)$			(178)$			(179)$		
(183) $			(184) $			(185) $		
(189)$			(190)$			(191)$		
(195)			(196)			(197)		

earnings and shares from the mergers completed in the fiscal year of the merger covered by this data sheet, but should exclude earnings and shares resulting from mergers in the following two fiscal years.

3. Please supply the following data for the acquired company. All figures should exclude the buying company.
   (a) Three fiscal years preceding the acquisition as presented in most recent published form prior to the merger.
   (b) Year of acquisition: (1) period from beginning of acquired company's fiscal year to the date of the acquisition;

	(a) 3 years prior to acquisition Fiscal year ending								
	(198) Month	Day	Year	(199) Month	Day	Year	(200) Month	Day	Year
Income Statement Items									
Sales	(203)$			(204)$			(205)$		
Net income before extraordinary items and amortization of goodwill	(211) $			(212) $			(213) $		
Extraordinary items	(219) $			(220) $			(221) $		
Amortization of goodwill	(227) $			(228) $			(229) $		
*Earnings per share	(235) $			(236) $			(237) $		
*Fully-diluted earnings per share (per APB Opinion 15)	(243) $			(244) $			(245) $		
Balance Sheet Items									
Total assets	(251)$			(252)$			(253)$		
Goodwill	(259) $			(260) $			(261) $		
Stockholders' equity	(267)$			(268)$			(269)$		
*Common shares outstanding	(275)			(276)			(277)		

* Supply this data subsequent to acquisition only if the acquired company continued to have shareholders outside of the buying company.

4. Please indicate the extent to which the buying company's financial statements had to be restated for its three fiscal years prior to the merger as a result of the acquisition described in this data sheet. If pooling accounting was used and the buying and the acquired companies had the same fiscal year, these data should be identical to those in section (a) of question 3 and if such is the case, this question may be omitted.

	Three fiscal years preceding the acquisition Fiscal year ending								
	(283) Month	Day	Year	(284) Month	Day	Year	(285) Month	Day	Year
Income Statement Items									
Sales	(286)$			(287)$			(288)$		
Net income before extraordinary items	(289) $			(290) $			(291) $		
Extraordinary items	(292) $			(293) $			(294) $		
Earnings per share	(295) $			(296) $			(297) $		
Fully-diluted earnings per share (per APB Opinion 15)	(298) $			(299) $			(300) $		
Balance Sheet Items									
Total assets	(301)$			(302)$			(303)$		
Goodwill	(304) $			(305) $			(306) $		
Stockholders' equity	(307)$			(308)$			(309)$		
Common shares outstanding	(310)			(311)			(312)		

5. Please supply the following data for the 12 months or 4 quarters immediately preceding the acquisition for both the buying and acquired company:

	Buying Company	Acquired Company
Net income before extraordinary items	(313) $	(314) $
Extraordinary items	(315) $	(316) $
Common shares outstanding	(317)	(318)
Earnings per share (as reported)	(319) $	(320) $

(2) period from date of acquisition to end of buying company's fiscal year; (3) amounts included in financial statements of the buying company in the year of the merger.

(c) Performance of the acquired company for two fiscal years subsequent to the merger.

(1) From beginning of acquired company's FY to date of acquisition	(2) From date of acquisition to end of buying company's fiscal year	(3) Amounts included in statements of buying company	(201) __ __ __ (202) __ __ __ Month Day Year Month Day Year					
(206)$_,_–,_–_–__	(207)$_,_–,_–_–__	(208)$_,_–,_–_–__	(209)$_,_–,_–_–__	(210)$_,_–,_–_–__
(214) $_,_–,_–_–__	(215) $_,_–,_–_–__	(216) $_,_–,_–_–__	(217) $_,_–,_–_–__	(218) $_,_–,_–_–__
(222) $_,_–,_–_–__	(223) $_,_–,_–_–__	(224) $_,_–,_–_–__	(225) $_,_–,_–_–__	(226) $_,_–,_–_–__
(230) $_,_–,_–_–__	(231) $_,_–,_–_–__	(232) $_,_–,_–_–__	(233) $_,_–,_–_–__	(234) $_,_–,_–_–,__
(238) $_,_–,_	(239) $_,_–,_	(240) $_,_–,_	(241) $_,_–,_	(242) $_,_–,_
(246) $_,_–,_	(247) $_,_–,_	(248) $_,_–,_	(249) $_,_–,_	(250) $_,_–,_
(254)$_,_–,_–_–__	(255)$_,_–,_–_–__	(256)$_,_–,_–_–__	(257)$_,_–,_–_–__	(258)$_,_–,_–_–__
(262) $_,_–,_–_–__	(263) $_,_–,_–_–__	(264) $_,_–,_–_–__	(265) $_,_–,_–_–__	(266) $_,_–,_–_–__
(270)$_,_–,_–_–__	(271)$_,_–,_–_–__	(272)$_,_–,_–_–__	(273)$_,_–,_–_–__	(274)$_,_–,_–_–__
(278) _,_–,_–_–__	(279) _,_–,_–_–__	(280) _,_–,_–_–__	(281) _,_–,_–_–__	(282) _,_–,_–_–__

(b) Year of Acquisition covers columns (1), (2), (3); (c) Two fiscal years subsequent to acquisition — Fiscal year ending.

---

6. Please supply the following data regarding stock dividends, stock splits and the sale for cash of common stock and securities convertible into common stock during the period 1964-1969.

A. Stock dividends and splits

Record date Month Day Year	Dividend (D) or Split (S)	Percentage increase in shares outstanding (For example a 3 for 2 stock split is a 50% increase in shares outstanding)
(321)___ __ __ __	—	(322)___ __ __ _%
(323)___ __ __ __	—	(324)___ __ __
(325)___ __ __ __	—	(326)___ __ __
(327)___ __ __ __	—	(328)___ __ __
(329)___ __ __ __	—	(330)___ __ __
(331)___ __ __ __	—	(332)___ __ __
(333)___ __ __ __	—	(334)___ __ __
(335)___ __ __ __	—	(336)___ __ __
(337)___ __ __ __	—	(338)___ __ __

B. Sales for cash

Date of Sale Month Day Year	Type of Security C—Common stock D—convertible debt P—convertible preferred W—debt with warrants O—other	Interest or Pfd. Dividend rate (as % of par) if applicable	No. of common shares (or no. common shares issuable on conversion)	Proceeds
(339)___ __ __ ___	—	__ _% (340)___,__–__–__	(341)$___,__–,__–__–__
(342)___ __ __ ___	—	__ _% (343)___,__–__–__	(344)$___,__–,__–__–__
(345)___ __ __ ___	—	__ _% (346)___,__–__–__	(347)$___,__–,__–__–__
(348)__ __ ___	—	__ _% (349)___,__–__–__	(350)$___,__–,__–__–__
(351)___ __ __ ___	—	__ _% (352)___,__–__–__	(353)$___,__–,__–__–__
(354)__ __ ___	—	__ _% (355)___,__–__–__	(356)$___,__–,__–__–__
(357)__ __ ___	__,	__ _% (358)___,__–__–__	(359)$___,__–,__–__–__

APPENDIX B

QUESTIONNAIRE FOR CHARTERED FINANCIAL ANALYSTS

Note: The first part of this questionnaire was sent to all CFAs. The rest of the questionnaire contained a case (General Precision Instruments Corp.) describing a business combination. The accounting treatment of the combination was varied three ways with each variation presented as a complete case to one-third of the CFAs.

1. The following exhibit shows certain financial data for the Great Company which acquired the Little Company on June 30, 19x2 in exchange for 13,000 shares of its common stock. Prior to that date, 100,000 shares of Great Company common stock was outstanding and on June 30, the stock traded at $40 per share. Part A below shows this combination accounted for as a pooling of interest while Part B shows the same companies combined on a purchase accounting basis with 40 year amortization of goodwill. In which part is the data presented in a more meaningful fashion from an analyst's viewpoint?

Part A better .... Part B better .... No difference ....

Why do you feel this way?

Great Company	Part A			
	19x1 as. orig. reptd.	*19x1 restated*	*19x2*	*19x3*
Book value (000)	$920	$1,117	$1,292	$1,505
Net income (000)	$135	$ 157	$ 185	$ 213
Earnings per share	$1.35	$1.39	$1.64	$1.89

Note: Great Company acquired Little Company on June 30, 19x2 by the issuance of 13,000 shares of common stock. The combination was accounted for as a pooling of interests. The earnings of Little Company prior to the date of acquisition in 19x2 totalled $12,500 while the earnings of Great Company for that six month period amounted to $80,000.

Great Company	Part B		
	19x1	19x2	19x3
Book value (000)	$920	$1,612	$1,817
Net income (000)	$135	$ 168	$ 205
Earnings per share	$1.35	$1.58	$1.81

Note: Great Company acquired Little Company on June 30, 19x2 in exchange for 13,000 shares of its stock having a market value of $520,000 on that date. The combination was accounted for as a purchase and the excess of price paid over assets acquired totalled $320,000 which is being amortized on a straight line basis over 40 years. Had the companies been combined for the entire year, net income on a pro forma basis would have been $177,000 or $1.55 per share. Pro forma net income for the year 19x1 reflecting the combined operations of the two companies amounted to $149,000 or $1.32 per share.

2. If goodwill is recorded on the books of the acquiring company in an acquisition, do you believe it should be amortized as a charge against earnings?

.... yes

.... no

Why do you feel this way?

a. If a company does not amortize goodwill, would you do so in computing earnings for analytical purposes?

.... yes

.... no

If you would not adjust earnings, would you apply a lower price/earnings multiple to the company's earnings for purposes of valuation than you would if it did amortize?

.... yes

.... no

b. If a company does amortize goodwill, would you eliminate (by adding back) amortization in computing earnings for analytical purposes?

.... yes

.... no

If you would not adjust earnings, would you apply a higher price/earnings multiple to the company's earnings for purposes of valuation than you would if it did not amortize?

.... yes

.... no

3. On the following four pages, certain data is presented about General Precision Instrument Corp. On the basis of this information, what value per share would you place upon the common stock of the company on the following end-of-fiscal-year dates:

a. September 30, 1967 ....

b. September 30, 1966 (in making this estimate, assume that you are at that point in time and that therefore you do not have 1967 data available) ....

Within what range are you quite certain that GPI stock would trade on those dates (i.e. chances that the stock would trade outside this range are less than 1 in 10 in your judgment)

a. September 30, 1967 .... to ....

b. September 30, 1966 .... to ....

General Precision Instrument Corp.

General Precision Instrument Corp. (GPI) manufactures and sells instruments, equipment and systems used in precision measurement, integrated circuit production and vacuum processing and welding materials. GPI also performs advanced research, development and engineering services, principally for government agencies. The Company's products and services are sold in a cross-section of technically oriented markets including electronics, aerospace, metals process control, and optical data processing.

In 1965, GPI acquired Scientific Apparatus Inc. (SAI) which primarily manufactures laboratory apparatus and analytical instruments. SAI's customers include educational institutions, research facilities, industrial laboratories and hospitals. Following the acquisition of SAI, GPI's sales were spread among four major markets as follows:

Laboratory apparatus and equipment	35%
Industrial equipment and products	25
Contract research and development	23
Instruments	17
	100%

In the industrial equipment market, GPI has had considerable success with its GPI Photorepeater, an important instrument in the photomask production facility of major integrated circuit manufacturers.

In Questionnaire I only—Purchase without amortization

GPI paid approximately $13,221,000 to purchase all the common shares of SAI. In order to raise this sum GPI sold 585,000 shares of Common Stock for $16.75 per share and issued $7,020,000 of 5½% Notes due 1972. The proceeds of these offerings in excess of the amount required to complete the purchase of SAI were used to reduce the Company's short term borrowings.

The acquisition of SAI was treated as a purchase for accounting purposes and accordingly net income of SAI was included in the accounts of GPI from the date of acquisition only. Thus, the consolidated statement of income for the year ended September 30, 1965 does not include the operations of SAI which was purchased on October 5, 1965 although a pro-forma statement showing the companies together is also presented in the exhibits. In the fiscal year ended June 30, 1965, SAI had Net Income of about $675,000 on sales of nearly $9,210,000. GPI does not intend to amortize the excess costs of investments in subsidiaries over net tangible assets acquired.

In Questionnaire II only—Purchase with amortization

GPI paid approximately $13,221,000 to purchase all the common shares of SAI. In order to raise this sum, GPI sold 585,000 shares of Common Stock for $16.75 per share and issued $7,020,000 of 5½% Notes due 1972. The proceeds of these offerings in excess of the amount required to complete the purchase of SAI were used to reduce the Company's short term borrowings.

The acquisition of SAI was treated as a purchase for accounting purposes and accordingly net income of SAI was included in the accounts of GPI from the date of acquisition only. Thus, the consolidated statement of income for the year ended September 30, 1965 does not include the operations of SAI which was purchased on October 5, 1965. In the fiscal year ended June 30, 1965, SAI had Net Income of about $675,000 on sales of nearly $9,210,000. GPI elected to amortize the excess cost of its investment over net tangible assets acquired on a straight-line basis over 40 years.

In Questionnaire III only—Pooling of Interests

During 1965 GPI issues $6,500,000 of 5½% Notes due 1972 and with the proceeds reduced short term borrowings and purchased treasury stock. On October 5, 1965 GPI obtained all the common shares of SAI in exchange for 585,000 newly issued shares of common stock and 150,000 shares of treasury stock. Based upon the market value of GPI's common stock of $17.00 per share, GPI paid $12,695,000 for SAI. At the time of the exchange SAI had net book value of $2,906,492 and estimated fair market value of net tangible assets of $5,005,000. In its fiscal year ended June 30, 1965, SAI had net income of $675,000 on sales of $9,210,000.

The acquisition of SAI was treated as a pooling of interests for accounting purposes. Accordingly, GPI's financial statements for the fiscal years ended September 30, 1964 and September 30, 1965 include the accounts of SAI.

During 1966 and 1967, the stock market was very strong. The high and low of the Dow Jones Industrial Average was 985 - 778 in 1966 and 923 - 830 in 1967. At September 30, 1966, the current market price/earnings multiple (based on the S & P 500 index) was 13.9 while at September 30, 1967 it stood at 17.8. The economy at that time was enjoying a period of great prosperity, partly as a result of the build-up of the war in Vietnam. Although GPI did not sell equipment which was directly used by the United States military in Vietnam, the Company nevertheless benefited indirectly. Military spending on Research and Development associated with the war in Vietnam rose sharply during 1965-1967. GPI was a direct beneficiary of this increased R & D spending. In addition, the stocks of those companies that were in any way associated with the manufacture of integrated circuits were extremely popular. These were the two most important factors in what one analyst called the 'mystique' of GPI.

GPI's stock is listed on the American Stock Exchange. Prior to the acquisition of SAI, the price range of the common stock was as follows:

Period:	High	Low
1964	31½	14¾
1965 (through Sept. 28)	21	14

GPI's stock closed at 17 on September 28, 1965.

The Company has never paid dividends on its common stock and feels that in the future all of its earnings will continue to be retained for the needs of the business.

GENERAL PRECISION INSTRUMENT CORP.

Comparative Income Statements
as Shown in the Three Questionnaires
Years Ended September 30. (Amounts in thousands)

Questionnaire I—Purchase without amortization

	1967	1966	Pro forma 1965	1965	1964
Net Sales	$31,335	$26,699	$23,334	$13,648	$12,995
Operating Costs & Expenses:					
Costs of Sales	23,611	19,874	17,781	11,015	10,819
Selling & G & A Expenses	3,416	3,247 ·	2,746	1,339	1,086
	27,027	23,121	20,527	12,354	11,905
Operating Profit	4,308	3,578	2,807	1,294	1,090
Interest:					
Interest on long term Debt	505	515	524	160	7
Other	80	—	(20)	—	72
	585	515	504	160	79
Income before Federal Income Tax	3,723	3,063	2,303	1,134	1,011
Federal Income Tax:					
Current	1,899	1,538	1,105	572	516
Deferred (Pre-paid)	—	(95)	—	(20)	(17)
	1,899	1,443	1,105	522	499
Net Income	$ 1,824	$ 1,620	$ 1,198	$ 598	$ 512
Per Share Common Stock	$1.47	$1.31	$ .98	$. 90	$ .80
Shares Outstanding (thousands)	1,238	1,235	1,232	647	640

Questionnaire II—Purchase with amortization

	1967	1966	Pro forma 1965	1965	1964
Net Sales	$31,335	$26,699	$23,334	$13,648	$12,995
Operating Costs & Expenses:					
Costs of Sales	23,611	19,874	17,781	11,015	10,819
Selling & G & A Expenses	3,416	3,247	2,746	1,339	1,086
	27,027	23,121	20,427	12,354	11,905
Operating Profit	4,308	3,578	2,807	1,294	1,090
Amortization of Goodwill	206	206	—	—	—
Interest:					
Interest on long term Debt	505	515	524	160	7
Other	80	—	(20)	—	72
	791	721	504	160	79
Income before Federal Income Tax	3,517	2,857	2,303	1,134	1,011
Federal Income Tax:					
Current	1,899	1,538	1,105	572	516
Deferred	—	(95)	—	(20)	(17)
	1,899	1,443	1,105	522	499
Net Income	$ 1,618	$ 1,414	$ 1,198	$ 582	$ 512
Per Share Common Stock	$1.31	$1.14	$ .98	$ .90	$ .80
Shares Outstanding (thousands)	1,238	1,235	1,232	647	640

GENERAL PRECISION INSTRUMENT CORP.

Comparative Income Statement for Questionnaire III

(Pooling of Interests)

	1967	1966	1965	As restated 1964	As reported 1964
Net Sales	$31,335	$26,699	$23,334	$21,520	$12,995
Operating Costs & Expenses:					
Costs of Sales	23,481	19,744	17,651	16,433	10,819
Selling & G & A Expenses	3,416	3,247	2,746	2,719	1,086
	26,897	22,991	20,397	19,152	11,905
Operating Profit	4,438	3,708	2,937	2,368	1,090
Interest:					
Interest on long-term debt ..	505	515	524	524	7
Other	80	—	(20)	72	72
	585	515	504	596	79
Income before Federal Income tax	3,853	3,193	2,433	1,772	1,011
Federal Income Tax:					
Current	1,964	1,603	1,170	889	516
Deferred (pre-paid)	—	(95)	—	(17)	(17)
	1,964	1,508	1,170	872	499
Net Income	$ 1,899	$ 1,685	$ 1,263	$ 900	$ 512
Earnings per share	$1.53	$1.36	$1.02	$ .73	$ .80
Shares Outstanding (thousands) ..	1,238	1,235	1,232	1,232	640

GENERAL PRECISION INSTRUMENT CORP.

Balance Sheet for Questionnaire I
(Purchase without amortization)

Years Ended September 30
(Amounts in Thousands)

Assets	1967	1966	Pro forma 1965	1964
Current Assets:				
Cash	$ 2,213	$ 1,699	$ 1,206	$ 274
Accounts Receivable	5,391	4,260	3,628	2,603
Unbilled Contract Costs	1,808	2,019	1,567	NA
Inventories—Lower Cost (FIFO) or mkt.				
Raw Materials	2,154	1,628	1,099	—
Work in Progress	2,839	2,254	1,791	—
Finished goods	1,513	1,141	1,225	—
	6,506	5,023	4,115	1,320
Prepaid Expenses	406	365	285	127
Total Current Assets	16,324	13,366	10,801	4,324
Plant, Property & Equipment:				
Land & Land Improvements	317	280	314	—
Buildings	362	346	771	—
Machinery & Equipment	3,728	3,472	3,446	—
Leasehold & Improvements	1,854	1,824	1,700	—
	6,261	5,922	6,231	—
Less Accumulated Depreciation	1,704	1,289	943	—
Net Plant, Property & Equipment	4,557	4,633	5,288	1,931
Excess of Cost of Investment in Subs. over Net tangible assets acquired	8,246	8,246	8,246	—
Prepaid Federal Income Tax (Net of deferred)	226	203	108	294
Total Assets	$29,353	$26,448	$24,443	$ 6,549
Liabilities				
Current Liabilities:				
Notes Payable to Bank	$ 2,210	$ 1,950	$ 1,300	$ 557
Accounts payable	1,546	911	924	651
Federal Income Tax	1,158	896	662	400
Salaries & Wages	556	549	435	—
Taxes other than Federal Income	202	134	169	—
Other accrued Liabilities	1,032	924	701	576
Long Term debt due w/in one year	524	471	297	—
Total Current Liabilities	7,228	5,835	4,488	2,184
Long Term Debt due after one year	5,937	6,581	7,483	1,260
Stockholders' Equity				
Common Stock $.60 pv. 7,000,000 auth.	742	741	739	387
Capital in Excess of par value	10,373	9,902	9,865	1,235
Retained Earnings	5,073	3,389	1,868	1,483
Total Stockholders' Equity	16,188	14,032	12,472	3,105
Total Liabilities	$29,353	$26,448	$24,443	$ 6,549

GENERAL PRECISION INSTRUMENT CORP.

Balance Sheet for Questionnaire II
(Purchase with amortization)
Years Ended September 30
(Amounts in Thousands)

Assets	1967	1966	Pro forma 1965	1964
Current Assets:				
Cash	$ 2,213	$ 1,699	$ 1,206	$ 274
Accounts Receivable	5,391	4,260	3,628	2,603
Unbilled Contract Costs	1,808	2,019	1,567	NA
Inventories—Lower Cost (FIFO) or mkt.				
Raw Materials	2,154	1,628	1,099	—
Work in Progress	2,839	2,254	1,791	—
Finished goods	1,513	1,141	1,225	—
	6,506	5,023	4,115	1,320
Prepaid Expenses	406	365	285	127
Total Current Assets	16,324	13,366	10,801	4,324
Plant, Property & Equipment:				
Land & Land Improvements	317	280	314	—
Buildings	362	346	771	—
Machinery & Equipment	3,728	3,472	3,446	—
Leasehold & Improvements	1,854	1,824	1,700	—
	6,261	5,922	6,231	—.
Less Accumulated Depreciation	1,704	1,289	943	—
Net Plant, Property & Equipment	4,557	4,633	5,288	1,931
Excess of Cost of Investment in Subs. over Net tangible assets acquired	7,834	8,040	8,246	—
Prepaid Federal Income Tax (Net of deferred)	226	203	108	294
Total Assets	$28,941	$26,242	$24,443	$ 6,549

Liabilities	1967	1966	Pro forma 1965	1964
Current Liabilities:				
Notes Payable to Bank	$ 2,210	$ 1,950	$ 1,300	$ 557
Accounts payable	1,546	911	924	651
Federal Income Tax	1,158	896	662	400
Salaries & Wages	556	549	435	—
Taxes other than Federal Income	202	134	169	—
Other accrued Liabilities	1,032	924	701	576
Long Term debt due w/in one year	524	471	297	—
Total Current Liabilities	7,228	5,835	4,488	2,184
Long Term Debt due after one year	5,937	6,581	7,483	1,260
Stockholders' Equity				
Common Stock $.60 pv. 7,000,000 auth.	742	741	739	387
Capital in Excess of par value	10,373	9,902	9,865	1,235
Retained Earnings	4,661	3,183	1,868	1,483
Total Stockholders' Equity	15,776	13,826	12,472	3,105
Total Liabilities	$28,941	$26,242	$24,443	$ 6,549

GENERAL PRECISION INSTRUMENT CORP.

Balance Sheet for Questionnaire III
(Pooling of Interests)
Years Ended September 30
(Amounts in Thousands)

Assets	1967	1966	1965	As restated 1964	As reported 1964
Current Assets:					
Cash	$ 2,213	$ 1,699	$ 1,206	$ 839	$ 274
Accounts Receivable	5,391	4,260	3,628	3,227	2,603
Unbilled Contracts Costs	2,208	2,319	2,167	1,752	NA
Inventories — Lower FIFO cost or market					
Raw Materials	2,154	1,628	1,099	—	—
Work in Progress	2,839	2,254	1,791	—	—
Finished Goods	1,513	1,141	1,225	—	—
	6,506	5,023	4,115	3,815	1,320
Prepaid Expenses	406	365	285	203	127
Total Current Assets	16,724	13,666	11,401	9,836	4,324
Plant Property & Equipment:					
Land & Land improvements	617	580	314	298	—
Buildings	1,198	1,175	1,474	1,771	—
Machinery & Equipment	2,368	2,172	2,146	1,965	—
Leasehold Improvements	1,086	1,056	932	756	—
	5,269	4,983	4,866	3,790	—
Less Accumulated Depreciation	1,314	1,029	813	677	—
Net Plant, Property & Equipment	3,955	3,954	4,053	4,113	1,931
Prepaid Federal Income Tax (net of deferred)	224	203	108	294	294
Total Assets	$20,903	$16,923	$15,562	$14,243	$ 6,549

Liabilities	1967	1966	1965	As restated 1964	As reported 1964
Current Liabilities:					
Notes Payable to Bank	$ 2,010	$ 1,750	$ 1,300	$ 1,100	$ 557
Accounts Payable	1,246	911	924	897	651
Federal Income Tax	748	531	597	530	400
Salaries & Wages	556	549	435	340	—
Taxes other than Federal Income	202	134	169	128	—
Other accrued Liabilities	632	429	401	319	576
Long Term debt due w/in one year	524	471	297	—	—
Total Current Liabilities	5,918	4,675	3,667	3,314	2,184
Long Term Debt	5,680	6,204	6,675	6,972	1,260
Stockholders' Equity					
Common Stock $.60 par value ..	742	741	739	739	387
Paid-in-capital	1,743	1,272	1,235	1,235	1,235
Retained Earnings	6,820	4,931	3,246	1,983	1,483
Total Stockholders' Equity ...	9,305	6,944	5,220	3,957	3,105
Total Liabilities & Equity	$20,903	$17,823	$15,562	$14,243	$ 6,549

GENERAL PRECISION INSTRUMENT

Income Statement

(Amounts in thousands)

Year ending September 30

	1967	1966	1965	As restated 1964	As reported 1964
Net Sales	$31,335	$26,699	$23,334	$12,995	$21,520
Operating Costs & Expenses:					
Costs of Sales	23,481	19,744	17,651	10,819	16,433
Selling & G & A Expenses	3,416	3,247	2,746	1,086	2,719
	26,897	22,991	20,397	11,905	19,152
Operating Profit	4,438	3,708	2,937	1,090	2,368
Interest:					
Interest on long-term debt	505	515	524	7	524
Other	80	—	(20)	72	72
	585	515	504	79	596
Income before Federal Income Tax	3,853	3,193	2,433	1,011	1,772
Federal Income Tax					
Current	1,964	1,603	1,170	516	889
Deferred (pre paid)	—	(95)	—	(17)	(17)
	1,964	1,508	1,170	499	872
Net Income	$ 1,899	$ 1,685	$ 1,263	$ 512	$ 900
Earnings per share	$1.53	$1.36	$1.02	$ .80	$ .73
Shares Outstanding (thousands) ..	1,238	1,235	1,232	640	1,232

EXPOSURE DRAFT

PROPOSED APB OPINION: BUSINESS COMBINATIONS AND INTANGIBLE ASSETS

FEBRUARY 23, 1970

Issued for comment from persons interested In Financial Reporting by the

ACCOUNTING PRINCIPLES BOARD

OF THE

AMERICAN INSTITUTE OF CERTIFIED PUBLIC ACCOUNTANTS

Comments should be received by May 15, 1970 and addressed to
Richard C. Lytle, Administrative Director, APB
at the Institute's offices, 666 Fifth Avenue, N. Y., N. Y. 10019

CONTENTS

INTRODUCTION

1. A business combination occurs when two or more corporations or a corporation and one or more unincorporated businesses are brought together into one entity. The single entity carries on the activities of previously separate, independent enterprises.

2. Two methods of accounting for business combinations are now accepted in practice—"purchase" and "pooling of interests"—and both are supported in pronouncements of the Board and its predecessor, the Committee on Accounting Procedure. The accounting treatment of a combination may affect significantly the reported financial position and net income of the combined corporation for both current and future periods. Accounting for combinations by the purchase method often involves accounting for goodwill acquired.

3. The Director of Accounting Research of the American Institute of Certified Public Accountants has published two studies on accounting for business combinations and the related goodwill: Accounting Research Study No. 5, A Critical Study of Accounting for Business Combinations, by Arthur R. Wyatt and Accounting Research Study No. 10, Accounting for Goodwill, by George R. Catlett and Norman O. Olson.[1] The two studies describe the origin and development of the purchase and pooling of interests methods of accounting for business combinations. The studies also cite the supporting authoritative pronouncements and their influences on accounting practices and evaluate the effects of practices on financial reporting. Accounting Research Study No. 10 emphasizes accounting for goodwill acquired in a business combination but also discusses accounting for goodwill developed internally.

[1] Accounting research studies are not statements of the Board or of the Institute but are published for the purpose of stimulating discussion on important accounting matters.

Scope and Effect of Opinion

4. The Board has considered the conclusions and recommendations of Accounting Research Studies Nos. 5 and 10, the discussions of the need for and appropriateness of the two accepted methods of accounting for business combinations, and proposals for alternative accounting procedures. It has also observed the present treatments of combinations in various forms and under differing conditions. The Board expresses in this Opinion its conclusions on the two subjects of accounting for business combinations and accounting for intangible assets, including goodwill acquired in business combinations.

5. This Opinion covers the combination of a corporation and another business enterprise which may be either incorporated or unincorporated; both incorporated and unincorporated enterprises are referred to in this Opinion as companies. The conclusions of this Opinion apply equally to business combinations in which one or more companies become subsidiary corporations, one company transfers its net assets to another, and each company transfers its net assets to a newly formed corporation. The term business combination in this Opinion excludes a transfer by a corporation of its net assets to a newly formed substitute corporate entity chartered by the existing corporation and a transfer of net assets between companies under common control, such as between a parent corporation and its subsidiary or between two subsidiary corporations of the same parent.

6. The conclusions of this Opinion modify previous views of the Board and its predecessor committee on the subjects of accounting for business combinations and intangible assets. This Opinion therefore supersedes the following Accounting Research Bulletins (ARB) and Opinions of the Accounting Principles Board (APB):

ARB No. 43, Chapter 5, Intangible Assets

ARB No. 48, Business Combinations

ARB No. 51, Consolidated Financial Statements, paragraphs 7, 8, and 9

APB Opinion No. 6, Status of Accounting Research Bulletins, paragraphs 12c, 15, and 22

APB Opinion No. 10, Omnibus Opinion—1966, paragraph 5.

Since this Opinion supersedes those existing pronouncements, paragraph 82 of this Opinion should be substituted for the reference to ARB No. 51 in paragraph 49 of APB Opinion No. 11.

Summary of Conclusions

7. Business Combinations. The Board concludes that the purchase method and the pooling of interests method are both acceptable in accounting for business combinations, although not as alternative accounting procedures. A business combination which meets specified conditions requires accounting by the pooling of interests method. The conditions include, among others, that each combining company in a business combination effected by exchanging voting common stock be at least one-third the size of each of the other combining companies as measured by relative voting common stock interests. A new basis of accounting is not permitted for a combination that meets the specified conditions, and the assets and liabilities of the combining companies are combined at their recorded amounts. All other business combinations should be accounted for as an acquisition of one or more companies by a corporation. The cost of an acquired company[2] should be determined by the principles of accounting for the acquisition of an asset. The cost of an acquired company should be allocated to the assets acquired and liabilities assumed based on the fair values of the identifiable individual assets and liabilities, and the remainder of the cost should be recorded as goodwill.

8. Intangible Assets. The Board concludes that a corporation should

[2] The cost of an acquired company is the acquiring corporation's cost of the entire enterprise acquired.

record as assets the costs of intangible assets acquired from others, including goodwill acquired in a business combination. A corporation may record as assets the costs incurred to develop identifiable intangible assets but should write off as incurred the costs to develop intangible assets which are not specifically identifiable, such as goodwill. The Board also concludes that the cost of each type of intangible asset should be amortized from date of acquisition by systematic charges to income over the period estimated to be benefited. The period of amortization should not, however, exceed forty years.

BUSINESS COMBINATIONS

Present Accounting and Its Development

9. *Development of Two Methods.* Most business combinations before World War II were classified either as a "merger," the acquisition of one company by another, or as a "consolidation," the formation of a new corporation. Accounting for both types of combinations generally followed traditional principles for the acquisition of assets or issuance of shares of stock. The accounting adopted by some new corporations was viewed as a precedent for the combining of retained earnings and of amounts of net assets recorded by predecessor corporations as retained earnings and net assets of a new entity.

10. Emphasis shifted after World War II from the legal form of the combination to distinctions between "a continuance of the former ownership or a new ownership" (ARB No. 40, paragraph 1). New ownership was accounted for as a purchase; continuing ownership was accounted for as a pooling of interests. Carrying forward the equity, including retained earnings, of the constituents became an integral part of the pooling of interests method. Significant differences between the purchase and pooling of interests methods accepted today are in the amounts ascribed to assets and liabilities at the time of

combination and the income reported for the combined enterprise.

11. *Purchase Method.*[3] The purchase method accounts for a business combination as the acquisition of one company by another. The acquiring corporation records at its cost the acquired assets less liabilities assumed. A difference between the cost of an acquired company and the sum of the fair values of tangible and identifiable intangible assets less liabilities is recorded as goodwill. The reported income of an acquiring corporation includes the operations of the acquired company after acquisition, based on the cost to the acquiring corporation.

12. The cost of goodwill acquired in a business combination either is retained as an asset until a loss of value is evident or is amortized over an arbitrary period. Chapter 5 of ARB No. 43, issued in 1953, provided that the cost of purchased goodwill should not be written off or reduced to a nominal amount at or immediately after acquisition.

13. *Pooling of Interests Method.*[3] The pooling of interests method accounts for a business combination as the uniting of the ownership interests of two or more companies by exchange of equity securities. No acquisition is recognized because the combination is accomplished without disbursing resources of the constituents. Own-

---

[3]This Opinion refers to the "purchase method of accounting" for a business combination because the term is widely used and generally understood. However, the more inclusive terms "acquire" (to come into possession of) and "acquisition" are generally used to describe transactions rather than the more narrow term "purchase" (to acquire by the payment of money or its equivalent). The broader terms clearly encompass obtaining assets by issuing stock as well as by disbursing cash and thus avoid the confusion and arguments that result from describing a stock transaction as a "purchase." This Opinion does not describe a business combination accounted for by the pooling of interests method of accounting as an "acquisition" because the meaning of the word is inconsistent with the method of accounting.

ership interests in the combining companies continue and the former bases of accounting are retained. The recorded assets and liabilities of the constituents are carried forward to the combined corporation at their recorded amounts. Income of the combined corporation includes income of the constituents for the entire fiscal period in which the pooling occurs. The reported income of the constituents for prior periods is combined and restated as income of the combined corporation.

14. The original concept of pooling of interests as a fusion of equity interests was modified in practice as use of the method expanded.[4] The method was first applied in accounting for combinations of affiliated corporations and then extended to some combinations of unrelated corporate ownership interests of comparable size. The method was later accepted for most business combinations in which common stock was issued. New and complex securities have been issued in recent business combinations and some combination agreements provide for additional securities to be issued later depending on specified events or circumstances. Most of the resulting combinations are accounted for as poolings of interests. Some combinations effected by both disbursing cash and issuing securities are now accounted for as a "part purchase, part pooling."

15. Some accountants believe that the pooling of interests method is the only acceptable method for a combination which meets the requirements for pooling. Others interpret the existing pronouncements on accounting for business combinations to mean that a combination which meets the criteria for a pooling of interests may alternatively be accounted for as a purchase.

---

[4]The origin, development, and application of the pooling of interests method of accounting are traced in Accounting Research Study No. 5 and summarized in Accounting Research Study No. 10.

Appraisal of Accepted Methods of Accounting

16. The pooling of interests method of accounting is applied only to business combinations effected by an exchange of stock and not to those involving primarily cash, other assets, or liabilities. Applying the purchase method of accounting to business combinations effected by paying cash, distributing other assets, or incurring liabilities is not challenged. Thus, those business combinations effected primarily by an exchange of equity securities present a question of choice between the two accounting methods.

17. The significantly different results of applying the purchase and pooling of interests methods of accounting to a combination effected by an exchange of stock stem from distinct views of the nature of the transaction itself. Those who endorse the pooling of interests method believe than an exchange of stock to effect a business combination is in substance a transaction between the combining stockholder groups and does not involve the corporate entities. The transaction therefore neither requires nor justifies establishing a new basis of accountability for the assets of the combined corporation. Those who endorse the purchase method believe that the transaction is an issue of stock by a corporation for consideration received from those who become stockholders by the transaction. The value of the consideration received is established by bargaining between independent parties, and the acquiring corporation accounts for the additional assets at their bargained—that is, current—values.

18. *Purchase Method.* The more important arguments expressing the advantages and disadvantages of the purchase method and some of the practical difficulties experienced in implementing it are summarized in paragraphs 19 to 27.

19. *An acquisition*—Those who favor the purchase method of accounting believe that one corporation acquires another company in almost every business combination. The acquisition of one company by another and the identities of the acquiring and acquired companies are usually obvious. Generally, one company in a business combination is clearly the dominant and continuing entity and one or more other companies cease to control their own assets and operations because control passes to the acquiring corporation. Identifying the acquirer may be difficult if the combining corporations are of relatively equal size. Some who favor the purchase method would permit the parties to designate one company as the acquirer, some would account for those combinations as new entities or mutual purchases, and some would favor pooling of interests accounting.

20. *A bargained transaction*—Proponents of purchase accounting hold that a business combination is a significant economic event which results from bargaining between independent parties. Each party bargains on the basis of his assessment of the current status and future prospects of each constituent as a separate enterprise and as a contributor to the proposed combined enterprise. The agreed terms of combination recognize primarily the bargained values and only secondarily the costs carried by the constituents. In fact, the recorded costs are not always known by the other bargaining party.

21. Accounting by the purchase method is essentially the same whether the business combination is effected by distributing assets, incurring liabilities, or issuing stock because issuing stock is considered an economic event as significant as distributing assets or incurring liabilities. A corporation must ascertain that the consideration it receives for stock issued is fair, just as it must ascertain that fair value is received for cash disbursed. Recipients of the stock similarly appraise the fairness of the transaction. Thus, a business combination is a bargained transaction regardless of the nature of the consideration.

22. *Reporting economic substance*—The purchase method adheres to traditional principles of accounting for the acquisition of assets. Those who support the purchase method of accounting for business combinations effected by issuing stock believe that an acquiring corporation accounts for the economic substance of the transaction by applying those principles and by recording:

a. All assets and liabilities which comprise the bargained cost of an acquired company, not merely those items previously shown in the financial statements of an acquired company.

b. The bargained costs of assets acquired less liabilities assumed, not the costs to a previous owner.

c. The fair value of the consideration received for stock issued, not the equity shown in the financial statements of an acquired company.

d. Retained earnings from its operations, not a fusion of its retained earnings and previous earnings of an acquired company.

e. Expenses and net income after an acquisition computed on the bargained cost of acquired assets less assumed liabilities, not on the costs to a previous owner.

23. *Defects attributed to purchase method*—Applying the purchase method to business combinations effected primarily by issuing stock may entail difficulties in measuring the cost of an acquired company. The reliability of the measure is diminished if neither the fair value of the consideration given nor the fair value of the property acquired is clearly evident. Measuring fair values of assets acquired is complicated by the presence of intangible assets or other assets which do not have discernible market prices. Goodwill and other unidentifiable intangible assets are difficult to value directly, and measuring the fair values of assets acquired for stock is easier

if the fair value of the stock issued is determinable. The excess of the fair value of stock issued over the sum of the fair values of the tangible and identifiable intangible assets acquired less liabilities assumed then indicates the value of unidentified intangible assets (goodwill) acquired.

24. However, the fair value of stock issued is not always objectively determinable. A market price may not be available for a newly issued security or for securities of a closely held corporation. Even an available quoted market price may not always be a reliable indicator of fair value of consideration received because the number of shares issued is relatively large, the market for the security is thin, the stock price is volatile, or other uncertainties influence the quoted price. Further, the determinable fair value of one security may not necessarily indicate the fair value of another similar, but not identical, security because their differences affect the fair value—for example, the absence of registration or an agreement which restricts a holder's ability to sell a security may significantly affect its fair value.

25. Those who oppose applying the purchase method to some or most business combinations effected by stock also challenge the theoretical merits of the method. They contend that the goodwill acquired is stated only by coincidence at the fair value which would be determined by direct valuation. The weakness is attributed not to measurement difficulties (direct valuation of goodwill is assumed) but to the underlying basis for an exchange of shares of stock. Bargaining in that type of transaction is normally based on the market prices of the equity securities. Market prices of the securities exchanged are more likely to be influenced by anticipated earnings capacities of the companies than by evaluations of individual assets. The number of shares of stock issued in a business combination is thus influenced by values attributed to goodwill of the acquirer as well

as the goodwill of the acquired company. Since the terms are based on the market prices of both stocks exchanged, measuring the cost of an acquired company by the market price of the stock issued may result in recording acquired goodwill at more or less than its fair value if determined directly.

26. A related argument is that the purchase method is improper accounting for a business combination in which a relatively large number of shares of stock is issued because it records the goodwill and fair values of only the acquired company. The critics of purchase accounting say that each group of stockholders of two publicly held and actively traded companies evaluates the other stock and the exchange ratio for stock issued is often predicated on relative market values. The stockholders and management of each company evaluate the goodwill and fair values of the other. Purchase accounting is thus viewed as illogical because it records goodwill and fair values of only one side of the transaction. Those who support this view prefer that assets and liabilities of both companies be combined at existing recorded amounts, but if one side is to be stated at fair values, they believe that both sides should be recorded at fair values.

27. Criticism of the purchase method is directed not only to the theoretical and practical problems of measuring goodwill in combinations effected primarily by stock but also to accounting for goodwill after the combination. Intangible assets acquired, including goodwill, often have indeterminate useful lives, and alternative methods of accounting are followed. Some corporations amortize the cost of acquired intangible assets over a short arbitrary period to reduce the amount of the asset as rapidly as practicable, while others retain the cost as an asset until evidence shows a loss of value and then record a material reduction in a single period. Selecting an arbitrary period of amortization is criticized because it may understate net income during the amortization

period and overstate later income. Retaining the cost as an asset is criticized because it may overstate net income before the loss of value is recognized and understate income in the period of write-off. Present accounting for goodwill is cited as an example of lack of uniformity because selecting among alternative methods is discretionary.

28. *Pooling of Interests Method.* The more important arguments expressing the advantages and disadvantages of the pooling of interests method and some of the practical difficulties experienced in implementing it are summarized in paragraphs 29 to 41.

29. *Validity of the concept—* Those who support the pooling of interests concept believe that a business combination arranged by an issuance of common shares is different from a purchase in that no corporate assets are disbursed to stockholders and the net assets of the issuing corporation are enlarged by the net assets of the corporation whose stockholders accept common stock of the combined corporation. There is no newly invested capital nor have owners withdrawn assets from the group since the stock of a corporation is not one of its assets. Accordingly, the net assets of the constituents remain intact but combined; the stockholder groups remain intact but combined. Aggregate income is not changed since the total resources are not changed. Consequently, the historical costs and earnings of the separate corporations are appropriately combined. In a business combination effected by exchanging stock, groups of stockholders combine their resources, talents, and risks to form a new entity which is designed to carry on in combination the previous businesses and to continue their earnings streams. The sharing of risks by the constituent stockholder groups is an important element in a business combination effected by exchanging stock. By pooling equity interests, each group continues to maintain risk elements of its former investment and they mutually exchange risks and benefits.

30. A pooling of interests transaction is regarded as being in substance an arrangement among stockholder groups. The fractional interests in the common enterprise are reallocated—risks are rearranged among the stockholder groups outside the corporate entity. A fundamental concept of entity accounting is that a corporation is separate and distinct from its stockholders. Elected managements represent the stockholders in the bargaining to effect the combination, but the groups of stockholders usually agree on final terms in the vote which approves or disapproves a combination. Stockholders sometimes disapprove a combination proposed by management, and tender offers sometimes succeed despite the opposition of management.

31. Each stockholder group in a pooling of interests is giving up its interests in assets formerly held but is receiving back an interest in some portion of the assets formerly held in addition to an interest in the assets of the other. The clearest example of this type of combination is one in which both stockholder groups surrender their shares and receive in exchange shares of a new corporation. The fact that one of the corporations usually issues its shares in exchange for those of the other does not alter the substance of the transaction. In a mutual exchange of this sort it should be recognized that the fair values of stocks that are surrendered reflect the tangible and intangible values as much as those that are received in exchange.

32. *Consistency with other concepts*—Proponents of pooling of interests accounting point out that the pooling theory was devéloped within the boundaries of the historical cost system and is compatible with it. Accounting as a pooling of interests for business combinations arranged through the issuance of common shares is based on existing accounting concepts and is not an occasion for revising historical cost data. Both constituents usually have elements of appreciation and of goodwill which

are recognized and offset, at least to some extent, in setting a share exchange ratio. The bargaining which takes place in setting an exchange ratio usually reflects the relative earning capacities (measured by historical cost accounts) of the constituents and frequently gives recognition to the relative market values of the two stocks, which in turn reflects this earning capacity, goodwill, or other values. Accounting recognition is given this bargaining by means of the new number of shares outstanding distributed in accordance with the bargained ratio, which has a direct effect on earnings per share after the combination.

33. *Usefulness of the concept*—Those who favor the pooling of interests method of accounting believe that the economic substance of a combination is best reflected by reporting operations up to the date of the exchange of shares based on the same historical cost information used to develop the separate operating results of each constituent and informative comparison with periods prior to the business combination is facilitated by maintaining historical costs as the basis of reporting combined operations subsequent to the combination.

34. *Application of the concept*—It has been observed that criteria for distinguishing between a pooling and a purchase have eroded over the years and that present interpretations of criteria have led to abuse. However, most accountants who support the pooling concept believe that criteria can be redefined satisfactorily to eliminate abuses. It is their view that the pooling of interests method of accounting for business combinations is justifiable on conceptual grounds and is a useful technique and therefore should not be abolished.

35. The concept of a uniting or fusing of stockholder groups on which pooling of interests accounting is based implies a broad application of the method because every combination effected by issuing stock rather than by disbursing cash or incurring debt is potentially

a pooling of interests unless the combination significantly changes the relative equity interests. However, so broad an application results in applying the pooling of interests method to numerous business combinations that many observers, including some who favor pooling of interests accounting, agree should be accounted for by the purchase method. Some proponents of pooling of interests accounting support a restriction on the difference in size of combining interests because a significant sharing of risk cannot occur if one combining interest is minor or because a meaningful mutual exchange does not occur if the combination involves a relatively small number of shares. Some others believe that a size restriction would aid in eliminating abuses of the pooling method in practice. Other proponents of the pooling of interests method, however, believe that there is no conceptional basis for a size restriction and that establishing a size restriction would seriously impair pooling of interests accounting.

36. *Defects attributed to pooling of interests method*—Those who oppose the pooling of interests method of accounting doubt that the method is supported by a concept. In their view it has become essentially a method of accounting for an acquisition of a company without recognizing the current fair values of the assets and goodwill underlying the transaction. The concept of a pooling of interests was described in general terms in the past—for example, as a continuity of equity interests or as a combination of two or more interests of comparable size. The descriptions tend to be contradictory. For example, accountants do not agree on whether or not relative size is part of the pooling of interests concept. Attempts to define the concept in terms of broad criteria for applying the accounting method have also been unsuccessful. At least, criteria which have been given as general guides to be weighed together rather than as firm rules to be followed have not achieved their purposes of clearly

delineating business combinations which are poolings of interests. Indeed, many opponents of the pooling of interests method of accounting believe that effective criteria cannot be found and that applying the method without effective criteria results in accounting as a pooling of interests for numerous business combinations which are clearly in economic substance the acquisition of one company by another.

37. Some critics point out that the method was first applied to combining interests of comparable size and that pronouncements on business combinations have never sanctioned applying pooling of interests accounting to all or almost all business combinations effected by exchanging stock. All pronouncements have indicated that a large disparity in the size of the combining interests is evidence that one corporation is acquiring another. The context shows that the 90 percent and 95 percent examples given in ARB No. 48 were intended as illustrations of disparities in size so large as to inhibit applying pooling of interests accounting and were not intended to be examples of boundaries between the pooling and purchase methods.

38. Other criteria restricting application of pooling of interests accounting, such as those prohibiting future disposals of stock received in a combination and providing for continuation of management, were added to the size restriction. Those criteria have, however, tended to weaken the concept of relative equality of the uniting interests because they are unilateral, that is, they are applied only to the stockholders and management of the "acquired" company.

39. The most serious defect attributed to pooling of interests accounting by those who oppose it, is that it does not accurately reflect the economic substance of the business combination transaction. They believe that the method ignores the bargaining which results in the combination and accounts only for the amounts previously shown in

accounts of the combining companies. The acquiring corporation does not record assets and values which usually influence the final terms of the combination agreement with consequent effects on subsequent balance sheets and income statements. The combined earnings streams, which are said to continue after a pooling of interests, can continue unchanged only if the cost of the assets producing those earnings is identical for the acquiring corporation and the acquired company. That coincidence rarely occurs because the bargaining is based on current fair values and not past costs.

40. Pooling of interests accounting is also challenged because the amount of assets acquired less liabilities assumed is determined without regard to the number of shares of stock issued. The result does not reflect the presumption that a corporation issues stock only for value received and, in general, the greater the number of shares issued, the larger the consideration to be recorded.

41. Traditional principles of accounting for acquisitions of assets encompass all business combinations because every combination is effected by distributing assets, incurring liabilities, issuing stock, or some blend of the three. Those who oppose the pooling of interests method believe that a departure from the traditional principles is justified only if evidence shows that financial statements prepared according to other principles either better reflect the economic significance of a combination or produce a superior financial report. In their opinion, the characteristics of a business combination do not justify departing from traditional principles of accounting to accommodate the pooling of interests method.

OPINION

42. The Board finds merit in both the purchase and pooling of interests methods of accounting and accepts neither method to the exclusion of the other. The Board concludes that the arguments in

favor of the purchase method of accounting are persuasive for most business combinations but that they are less persuasive if voting common stock is issued to effect a combination of companies of relatively the same size. The Board also concludes that arguments in favor of the pooling of interests method of accounting are persuasive if voting common stock is issued to effect a combination of companies of relatively the same size but less persuasive if the combining companies are of disparate size. Therefore, the Board concludes that most business combinations should be accounted for by the purchase method but that some combinations should be accounted for by the pooling of interests method. The two methods are not alternatives in accounting for the same business combination.

43. The Board believes that accounting for business combinations will be improved significantly by specifying the circumstances in which each method should be applied and the procedures which should be followed in applying each method. The distinctive conditions which require pooling of interests accounting are described in paragraphs 44 to 47, and combinations involving all of those conditions should be accounted for as described in paragraphs 48 to 62. All other business combinations should be treated as the acquisition of one company by another and accounted for by the purchase method as described in paragraphs 63 to 89.

44. *Conditions for Pooling of Interests Method.* A business combination which meets *all* of the conditions specified and explained in paragraphs 45 to 47 should be accounted for by the pooling of interests method. The conditions are classified by (1) attributes of the combining companies, (2) the manner of effecting the combining transaction, and (3) the absence of planned transactions.

45. *Combining companies* — The two conditions in this group relate to certain attributes of the combining companies, either individually or in relation to each other.

a. Each combining company has been an active, independent company for at least two years before the plan of combination is initiated.

This condition means that each company is not or has not been within the preceding two years a subsidiary or division of another corporation.

A plan of combination is initiated on the earlier of the date that a plan is announced or the date that stockholders of a combining company are notified in writing of an exchange offer.

b. Each combining company is not less than one-third the size of each other combining company, that is, each company is not more than three times the size of each of the other combining companies.

The size of a combining company is measured by its voting common stock ownership interest at the date the plan of combination is consummated. To compare sizes of combining companies, the number of shares of outstanding voting common stock of each company is expressed in terms of an equivalent number of shares of common stock of the resulting combined corporation. The equivalent number of shares of the combined corporation for each combining company is the number of shares that would be received by its stockholders if all of its outstanding voting common stock were exchanged in the combination.

For the size computations, the voting common stock ownership interest of a combining company includes the number of shares of common stock outstanding at the date the plan of combination is consummated plus those shares of stock of that company which were previously outstanding during the period beginning two years preceding the date the combination is initiated but were exchanged for a convertible debt security, convertible preferred stock, or other security which has the right to become common stock, all as restated in terms of its current outstanding stock.

46. *Combining transaction*—The six conditions in this group relate to the manner of effecting the combination.

a. The combination is effected in a single transaction or is completed in accordance with a specific plan within one year after the plan is initiated.

Alteration of the terms of exchange constitutes initiation of a new plan of combination.

A business combination completed in more than one year from the date of initiation of a plan meets this condition if the delay is beyond the control of the combining companies because proceedings of a regulatory authority or litigation prevents completing the combination.

b. A corporation offers and issues only common stock with rights identical to those of the majority of its outstanding voting common stock in exchange for substantially all of the voting common stock interest of another company at the date the plan of combination is consummated.

The plan to issue voting common stock in exchange for voting common stock may include provisions to distribute cash or other consideration for fractional shares, for shares held by dissenting stockholders, and the like but may not include a pro rata distribution of cash or other consideration. However, the total distributions of cash or other consideration may not exceed the limits described in the explanations of this condition.

An exchange of substantially all of the voting common stock for this condition means that 90 percent or more of the outstanding common stock of a combining company is exchanged between the dates the plan of combination is initiated and consummated[5] for the voting common stock issued by another corporation (issuing corporation) to effect the combination. However, 90 percent of the outstanding common stock of a combining company

is compared with the number of shares of stock exchanged for common stock reduced by the effects of certain treasury stock transactions and intercorporate investments in the stock being issued to effect the combination. Reductions relate to shares of common stock of the corporation issuing stock to effect the combination which are

(i) held as an investment by the other combining company at the date the plan of combination is initiated,

(ii) acquired by the other combining company after the date the plan of combination is initiated, and

(iii) acquired as treasury stock by the issuing corporation after the date the plan of combination is initiated.[6]

The number of shares of stock of the issuing corporation in the three categories are restated as the equivalent number of shares of the other combining company determined by the ratio of exchange of stock and the total is deducted from the number of shares of stock of the combining company which are exchanged. Condition (b) is not met if the reduced number of shares of stock exchanged is less than 90 percent of the outstanding common stock interest of the company at

[5]The shares of common stock exchanged between the two dates does not include shares of common stock of a combining company acquired by the issuing corporation before and held at the date the plan of combination is initiated, regardless of the form of consideration. Common stock held at March 1, 1970 results in an exception to the 90 percent minimum exchange and is explained in paragraph 113.

[6]The number of shares of treasury stock excludes those shares which a corporation acquired for purposes other than business combinations, such as stock option and compensation plans, providing (1) the stock is acquired under a systematic pattern of stock reacquisitions established at least two years before the plan of combination is initiated and (2) the number of shares is reasonable in relation to the number of shares reacquired before the plan of combination is initiated.

the date the plan of combination is consummated.[7]

The 90 percent minimum exchange applies to each combining company except the corporation that issues stock to effect the business combination. If a corporation issues stock for the stock of more than one combining company, a reduction for treasury stock acquired by the issuing corporation (iii above)

should be allocated to the exchanged shares of each combining company in proportion to the total number of shares of stock the issuing corporation could potentially issue in the combination.

A new corporation formed to issue its stock to effect the combination of two or more companies meets condition (b) if (1) the number of

shares of each company exchanged to effect the combination is not less than 90 percent of its voting common stock outstanding at the date the combination is consummated and (2) condition (b) would have been met had any one of the combining companies issued its stock to effect the combination on essentially the same basis. Several separate computations may be required for provision (2)—each of the combining companies in turn should be assumed to have issued stock to effect the combination. The assumed exchange of stock should be based on the ratios of exchange of stock of the individual companies for that of the new corporation. Each separate computation should recognize the applicable reductions in categories (i), (ii), and (iii). A combination effected through a new corporation meets provision (2) if at least one of the existing combining companies could have satisfied condition (b) by issuing its stock.

Condition (b) relates to issuing common stock for the common stock interests in another company. Hence, a corporation issuing stock to effect the combination may assume the debt securities of the other company or may exchange substantially identical securities or common stock for debt and other outstanding equity securities of the other combining company. An issuing corporation may also distribute cash to holders of debt and equity securities that either are callable or redeemable and may retire those securities.

A business combination effected by a transfer of the net assets of a company may meet condition (b) providing all of the net assets of the company at the date the plan is consummated are transferred for stock of the issuing corporation. The combining company may retain temporarily cash, receivables, or marketable securities to settle liabilities, contingencies, or items in dispute if the plan provides that the assets remaining after settlement are to be transferred to the corporation issuing the stock to effect the

---

[7]Computation of the 90 percent minimum exchange may be illustrated by an example.

Corporation A and Corporation B each have 20,000 shares of voting common stock outstanding on January 22, 1977. On that date Corp. A and Corp. B initiate a plan to combine by an exchange of one share of common stock of Corp. A for each two shares of common stock of Corp. B.

Corp. A issues 9,600 shares of its common stock to holders of 19,200 shares of Corp. B common stock on November 13, 1977. Corp. A pays cash for fractional shares equivalent to 100 shares of Corp. B common stock.

Other information:

–Corp. A acquired 300 shares of Corp. B common stock for stock in 1971. Corp. B bought 200 shares of Corp. A common stock for cash in 1976. Both investments are held on January 22, 1977. Corp. B bought 100 shares of Corp. A common stock for cash on July 19, 1977.

–Both companies regularly reacquire common stock for compensation plans. Corp. A has reacquired 500 shares each year from 1973 to 1976; Corp. B has reacquired 300 shares each year from 1971 to 1976. Corp. A reacquired 290 shares on June 4, 1977 and 600 shares on August 27, 1977, and Corp. B reacquired 200 shares on May 4, 1977.

	No. of Shares
Computations for condition (b):	
Common stock of Corp. B outstanding on November 13, 1977—	
Outstanding on date plan of combination is initiated	20,000
Treasury stock acquired on May 4, 1977	200
Outstanding on date plan is consummated	19,800
90 percent	17,820
Common stock of Corp. B acquired in exchange for voting common stock of Corp. A (excludes 100 shares acquired for cash, 300 shares acquired before date plan is initiated, and 200 shares remaining outstanding as minority interest)	19,200
Reduced by—	
Common stock of Corp. A held by Corp. B at date plan is initiated, restated as equivalent number of Corp. B shares in ratio of 2 to 1 (200 x 2) 400	
Common stock of Corp. A acquired by Corp. B after date plan is initiated, restated as equivalent number of Corp. B shares in ratio of 2 to 1 (100 x 2) 200	
Common stock of Corp. A acquired as treasury stock, less shares regularly reacquired for compensation, restated as equivalent number of Corp. B shares in ratio of 2 to 1 [(890 — 500) x 2] 780 1,380	
Computed number of shares of common stock for comparison with 90 percent minimum	17,820

The shares acquired in exchange for voting common stock of Corp. A equals at least 90 percent of the outstanding voting common stock interest of Corp. B at the date the plan is consummated. The condition that substantially all shares are exchanged is met.

combination. The stock issued to effect the combination must be all common stock unless both preferred and common stocks of the other combining company are outstanding at the date the plan is consummated. If so, the combination may be effected by issuing all common stock or by issuing common and preferred stock in the same proportions as the outstanding common and preferred stock equities of the other combining company. In addition, certain transactions in common stock of the combining companies are considered to affect the issue of stock to measure the condition on the same basis as an exchange of stock. First, the total number of shares of common stock issued to effect the combination should be divided between those applicable to the preferred stock equity and those applicable to the common stock ownership interest in the combining company if both types of securities are outstanding. Second, the number of shares of common stock applicable to the common stock ownership interest should be reduced for specified intercorporate investments and certain treasury stock transactions of the issuing corporation. Reductions comprise:

Shares of common stock of the corporation issuing stock to effect the combination which are

(i) held as an investment by the other combining company at the date the plan of combination is initiated,

(ii) acquired by the other combining company after the date the plan of combination is initiated, and

(iii) acquired as treasury stock by the issuing corporation after the date the plan of combination is initiated[8]

and shares of common stock of the combining company held as an investment by the issuing corporation at the date the plan of combination is initiated but restated as a number of shares of the issuing corporation based on the ratio of the number of out-

[8]Note 6, page 11.

standing shares of common stock of the combining company at the date the plan is consummated to the number of shares of common stock issued to transfer the assets which are applicable to the common stock ownership interest.

The reduced number of shares of stock must equal 90 percent or more of the number of shares issued for the common stock ownership interest of the combining company to meet condition (b).[9]

c. The relative interests of individual common stockholders in each of the combining com-

panies are not realigned by the exchange of securities to effect the combination.

This condition means that each individual common stockholder of each combining company receives a voting common stock interest exactly in proportion to his relative common stock interest before the combination is effected. Thus no common stockholder is denied or surrenders his potential share of a voting common stock interest in a combined corporation.

d. The voting rights to which the common stock ownership interests in the resulting com-

[9]An example of the computation assumes facts similar to those in note 7.

Corporation C and Corporation D each have 20,000 shares of voting common stock outstanding on January 22, 1977. On that date Corp. C and Corp. D initiate a plan to combine by a transfer of the net assets of Corp. D to Corp. C in exchange for 10,000 shares of common stock of Corp. C.

Corp. C issues 10,000 shares of its common stock to Corp. D on November 13, 1977.

Other information:

—Corp. C acquired 300 shares of Corp. D common stock for stock in 1971. Corp. D bought 200 shares of Corp. C common stock for cash in 1976. Both investments are held on January 22, 1977. Corp. D bought 100 shares of Corp C common stock for cash on July 19, 1977.

—Both companies regularly reacquire common stock for compensation plans. Corp. C has reacquired 500 shares each year from 1973 to 1976; Corp. D has reacquired 300 shares each year from 1971 to 1976. Corp. C reacquired 290 shares on June 4, 1977 and 600 shares on August 27, 1977, and Corp. D reacquired 200 shares on May 4, 1977.

		No. of Shares
Computations for condition (b):		
Common stock of Corp. C issued on November 13, 1977		10,000
90 percent		9,000
Common stock of Corp. C issued for net assets of Corp. D Reduced by—		10,000
Common stock of Corp. C held by Corp. D at date plan is initiated	200	
Common stock of Corp. C acquired by Corp. D after date plan is initiated	100	
Common stock of Corp. C acquired as treasury stock, less shares regularly reacquired for compensation (890—500)	390	
Common stock of Corp. D held by Corp. C at date plan is initiated, restated as equivalent number of Corp. C shares in ratio of 1.98 to 1 based on 19,800 shares of Corp. D stock outstanding on date plan is consummated (300÷1.98)	152	842
Computed issue of shares of common stock for comparison with 90 percent minimum		9,158

The reduced shares issued for the transfer of all net assets equals at least 90 percent of the shares issued and the condition is met.

bined corporation are entitled are exercisable by the stockholders; the stockholders are neither deprived nor restricted in exercising those rights for a period.

This condition is not met, for example, if shares of common stock issued to effect the combination are transferred to a voting trust.

e. A combining company other than the corporation issuing stock to effect the combination distributes no more than normal dividends and reacquires no more than a normal number of shares of common stock after the date the plan of combination is initiated.

The normality of dividends is determined in relation to earnings during the period and to the previous dividend policy for purposes of this condition. The normal number of shares of stock reacquired is determined by the pattern of reacquisitions of stock before the plan is initiated.

f. The combination is resolved at the date the plan is consummated and no provisions of the plan relating to the issue of securities or other consideration are pending.

This condition means that (1) the combined corporation does not agree to contingently issue additional shares of stock or distribute other consideration at a later date to the former stockholders of a combining company or (2) the combined corporation does not issue or distribute to an escrow agent common stock or other consideration which is to be either transferred to common stockholders or returned to the corporation at the time the contingency is resolved.

An exception to this condition is a provision that the number of shares of common stock issued to effect the combination may be revised for the later settlement of a contingency at a different amount than that recorded by a combining company.

47. *Absence of planned transactions*—The three conditions in this group relate to certain future transactions.

a. The combined corporation does not agree directly or indirectly to retire or reacquire all or part of the common stock issued to effect the combination.

b. The combined corporation does not enter into other financial arrangements for the benefit of the former stockholders of a combining company, such as a guaranty of loans secured by stock issued in the combination, which in effect negates the exchange of equity securities.

c. The combined corporation does not intend or plan to dispose of a significant part of the assets of the combining companies within two years after the combination except to eliminate duplicate facilities or excess capacity and those assets that would have been disposed of in the ordinary course of business of the separate company.

Pooling of Interests Method of Accounting

48. A business combination which meets all of the conditions in paragraphs 44 to 47 should be accounted for by the pooling of interests method. Appropriate procedures are described in paragraphs 49 to 62.

49. *Assets and Liabilities Combined.* The recorded assets and liabilities of the separate companies generally become the recorded assets and liabilities of the combined corporation. The combined corporation therefore recognizes those assets and liabilities recorded in conformity with generally accepted accounting principles by the separate companies at the date the combination is consummated.

50. The combined corporation records the historical-cost based amounts of the assets and liabilities of the separate companies because the existing basis of accounting

continues. However, the separate companies may have recorded assets and liabilities under differing methods of accounting and the amounts may be adjusted to the same basis of accounting if the change would otherwise have been appropriate for the separate company. A change in accounting method to conform the individual methods should be applied retroactively, and financial statements presented for prior periods should be restated.

51. *Stockholders' Equity Combined.* The stockholders' equities of the separate companies are also combined as a part of the pooling of interests method of accounting. The combined corporation records as capital the capital stock and capital in excess of par or stated value of outstanding stock of the separate companies. Similarly, retained earnings or deficits of the separate companies are combined and recognized as retained earnings of the combined corporation. The amount of outstanding shares of stock of the combined corporation at par or stated value may exceed the total amount of capital stock of the separate combining companies; the excess should be deducted first from the combined other contributed capital and then from the combined retained earnings. The combined retained earnings could be misleading if shortly before or as a part of the combination transaction one or more of the combining companies adjusted the elements of stockholders' equity to eliminate a deficit; therefore, the elements of equity before the adjustment should be combined.

52. A corporation which distributes treasury stock to effect a combination accounted for by the pooling of interests method should first account for the effective retirement of those shares of stock at the time of their distribution. The issuance of the shares for the common stock interests of the combining company is then accounted for the same as the issuance of previously unissued shares.

53. Accounting for common stock of one of the combining com-

panies which is held by another combining company at the date a combination is consummated depends on whether the stock is the same as that which is issued to effect the combination or is the same as the stock which is exchanged in the plan of combination. An intercorporate investment of a combining company in the common stock of the corporation issuing additional stock in a combination is in effect returned to the resulting combined corporation in the combination. The combined corporation should account for the investment as treasury stock. In contrast, an intercorporate investment in the common stock of other combining companies (not the one issuing stock in the combination) is an investment in stock that is exchanged in the combination for the common stock issued. The stock in that type of intercorporate investment is in effect eliminated in the combination. The combined corporation should account for that investment as stock retired as part of the combination.

54. *Reporting Combined Operations.* A corporation which applies the pooling of interests method of accounting to a combination should report results of operations for the period in which the combination occurs as though the companies had been combined as of the beginning of the period. Results of operations for that period thus comprises those of the separate companies from the beginning of the period to the date the combination is consummated and those of the combined operations from that date to the end of the period. A combined corporation should disclose in notes to financial statements the revenue, extraordinary items, and net income of each of the separate companies from the beginning of the period to the date the combination is consummated. The information relating to the separate companies may be as of the end of the interim period nearest the date that the combination is consummated.

55. Similarly, balance sheets and other financial information of the separate companies as of the beginning of the period should be presented as though the companies had been combined at that date. Financial statements and financial information of the separate companies presented for prior years should also be restated on a combined basis to furnish comparative information. All restated financial statements and financial summaries should indicate clearly that financial data of the previously separate companies are combined.

56. *Expenses Related to Combination.* All expenses related to effecting a business combination accounted for by the pooling of interests method should be deducted in determining the net income of the resulting combined corporation for the period in which the expenses are incurred. Thus, all costs to effect the combination and integrate the operations are expenses of the combined corporation and are not direct reductions of stockholders' equity. Those expenses include, for example, registration fees, costs of furnishing information to stockholders, fees of finders and consultants, salaries and other expenses related to services of employees, and costs and losses of combining operations of the previously separate companies and instituting efficiencies.

57. *Disposition of Assets After Combination.* A combined corporation may dispose of those assets of the separate companies which are duplicate facilities or excess capacity in the combined operations. Losses or estimated losses on disposal of specifically identified duplicate or excess facilities should be deducted in determining the net income of the resulting combined corporation. However, a loss estimated and recorded while a facility remains in service should not include the portion of the cost that is properly allocable to anticipated future service of the facility.

58. Profit or loss on other dispositions of assets of the previously separate companies may require special disclosure. Specific treatment of a profit or loss on those dispositions is warranted because the pooling of interests method of accounting would have been inappropriate (paragraph 47) if the combined corporation were committed or planned to dispose of a significant part of the assets of one of the combining companies. The Board therefore concludes that a combined corporation should disclose separately a profit or loss resulting from the disposal of a significant part of the assets of the previously separate companies, providing

the profit or loss is material in relation to the net income of the combined corporation and

the disposition is within two years after the combination is consummated.

The disclosed profit or loss, less applicable income tax effect, should be classified as an extraordinary item unless the disposals are part of customary business activities of the combined corporation.

59. *Date of Recording Combination.* A business combination accounted for by the pooling of interests method should be recorded as of the date the combination is consummated. Therefore, even though a business combination is consummated before one or more of the combining companies first issues its financial statements as of an earlier date, the financial statements should be those of the combining company only and not those of the resulting combined corporation. A combining company should, however, disclose in notes to financial statements the substance of a combination consummated before financial statements are issued and the effects of the combination on reported financial position and results of operations (paragraph 62). Earlier financial statements of the separate companies should be combined to present comparative financial statements in reports of the resulting combined corporation dated after a combination is consummated.

60. A corporation may have acquired common stock of another combining company as part of a business combination which has been initiated but not consummated

as of the date of financial statements. The corporation should record as an investment the common stock of the other combining company acquired before the statement date. Common stock acquired by disbursing cash or other assets or by incurring liabilities should be recorded at cost. Stock acquired in exchange for common stock of the issuing corporation should, however, be recorded at the proportionate share of underlying net assets as recorded by the other company at the date acquired if the corporation expects the combination to meet the conditions requiring the pooling of interests method of accounting. Until the appropriate method of accounting for the combination is known, the investment and net income of the investor corporation should include the proportionate share of earnings or losses of the other company.

61. *Disclosure of a Combination.* A combined corporation should disclose in its financial statements that a combination which is accounted for by the pooling of interests method occurred during the period. The basis of current presentation and restatements of prior periods may be disclosed in the financial statements by captions or by references to notes.

62. Notes to financial statements of a combined corporation for the period in which a business combination is accounted for by the pooling of interests method should disclose the following:

a. Name and brief description of the companies combined, except a corporation whose name is carried forward to the combined corporation.

b. Description and number of shares of stock issued in the business combination.

c. Method of accounting for the combination—that is, by the pooling of interests method.

d. Details of the results of operations of the previously separate companies for the period before the combination is consummated that are included in the current com-

bined net income (paragraph 54). The details should include revenue, extraordinary items, net income, and other changes in stockholders' equity.

e. Descriptions of the nature of adjustments of net assets of the combining companies to adopt the same accounting practices and of the effects of the changes on net income reported previously by the separate companies (paragraph 50).

f. Details of an increase or decrease in retained earnings from changing the fiscal year of a combining company. The details should include at least revenue, expenses, extraordinary items, net income and other changes in stockholders' equity.

g. Reconciliations of amounts of revenue and earnings previously reported by the corporation that issues the stock to effect the combination with the combined amounts currently presented in financial statements and summaries. A new corporation formed to effect a combination may instead disclose the earnings of the separate companies which comprise combined earnings for prior periods.

h. Details of the effects of a business combination consummated before the financial statements are issued but either incomplete as of the date of the financial statements or initiated after that date (paragraph 59). The details should include revenue, net income, earnings per share, and the effects of anticipated changes in accounting methods as if the combination had been consummated at the date of the financial statements (paragraph 50).

The information disclosed in notes to financial statements should also be furnished on a pro forma basis in materials on a proposed business combination which is given to stockholders of combining companies.

Purchase Method of Accounting

63. *Principles of Historical-Cost Accounting.* Accounting for a business combination by the purchase method should follow principles normally applicable under historical-cost accounting to recording acquisitions of assets and issuances of stock and to accounting for assets and liabilities after acquisition.

64. *Acquiring assets*—The general principles to apply the historical-cost basis of accounting to an acquisition of an asset depend on the nature of the transaction:

a. An asset acquired by exchanging cash or other corporate assets is recorded at cost—that is, at the amount of cash disbursed or the fair value[10] of other assets distributed.

b. An asset acquired by incurring liabilities is recorded at cost—that is, at the present value of the amounts to be paid.

c. An asset acquired by issuing shares of stock of the acquiring corporation is recorded at the fair value of the asset received—that is, shares of stock issued are recorded at the fair value of the consideration received for the stock.

The basis of accounting is that which is given (assets distributed or liabilities incurred) in the first two principles but that which is received in the third principle because a corporation issues stock to recognize equity contributions by owners.

65. The general principles must be supplemented to apply them in certain transactions. Thus, the fair value of an asset received for stock issued may not be reliably determinable, or the fair value of an asset acquired in an exchange may be more reliably determinable than

[10]In general, fair value implies a result equivalent to that of a cash transaction. That is, the fair values of assets received or distributed are approximately the amounts of cash that would have been paid or received between independent parties.

the fair value of a noncash asset given up. Restraints on measurement have led to the practical rule that assets acquired for other than cash, including shares of stock issued, should be stated at "cost" when they are acquired and "cost may be determined either by the fair value of the consideration given or by the fair value of the property acquired, whichever is the more clearly evident".[11] "Cost" is the term accountants apply to the amount at which an entity records an asset at the date it is acquired whatever its manner of acquisition, and that "cost" forms the basis for historical-cost accounting.

66. *Allocating cost* — Acquiring assets in groups requires not only ascertaining the cost of the assets as a group but also allocating the cost to the individual assets which comprise the group. The cost of a group is determined by the principles described in paragraphs 64 and 65. The cost of the group is then assigned to the individual assets acquired on the basis of the fair value of each. A difference between the sum of the fair values of the tangible and identifiable intangible assets acquired less liabilities assumed and the cost of the group is evidence of unspecified intangible values.

67. *Accounting after acquisition*—The nature of an asset and not the manner of its acquisition determines an acquirer's subsequent accounting for the cost of that asset. The basis for measuring the cost of an asset—whether amount of cash paid, fair value of an asset received or given up, amount of a liability incurred, or fair value of stock issued—has no effect on the subsequent accounting for that cost, which is retained as an asset, depreciated, amortized, or otherwise matched with revenue.

68. *Acquiring Corporation.* A corporation which distributes cash or other assets or incurs liabilities to obtain the assets or stock of

[11]ARB No. 24; the substance was retained in slightly different words in Chapter 5 of ARB No. 43 and ARB No. 48.

another company is clearly the acquirer. The identities of the acquirer and the acquired company are usually evident in a business combination effected by the issue of stock. The acquiring company normally issues the stock and commonly is the larger company. The acquired company may, however, survive as the corporate entity, and the nature of the negotiations sometimes clearly indicate that a smaller corporation acquires a larger company. If a new corporation is formed to issue stock to effect a business combination to be accounted for by the purchase method, one of the existing combining companies should be considered the acquirer. The Board concludes that presumptive evidence of the acquiring corporation in combinations effected by an exchange of stock is obtained by identifying the former common stockholder interests of a combining company which either retain or receive the larger portion of the voting rights in the combined corporation. That corporation should be treated as the acquirer unless other evidence clearly indicates that another corporation is the acquirer.

69. *Determining Cost of an Acquired Company.* The same accounting principles apply to determining the cost of assets acquired individually, those acquired in a group, and those acquired in a business combination. A cash payment by a corporation measures the cost of acquired assets less liabilities assumed. Similarly, the fair values of other assets distributed, such as marketable securities or properties, and the fair value of liabilities incurred by an acquiring corporation measure the cost of an acquired company. The present value of a debt security represents the fair value of the liability, and a premium or discount should be recorded for a debt security issued with an interest rate fixed materially above or below the rate for an otherwise comparable security.

70. The distinctive attributes of preferred stocks make some issues similar to a debt security while others possess common stock characteristics, with many gradations between the extremes. Determining cost of an acquired company may be affected by those characteristics. For example, the fair value of a nonvoting, nonconvertible preferred stock which lacks characteristics of common stock may be determined by comparing the specified dividend and redemption terms with comparable securities and by assessing market factors. Thus although the principle of recording the fair value of consideration received for stock issued applies to all equity securities, senior as well as common stock, the cost of a company acquired by issuing senior equity securities may be determined in practice on the same basis as for debt securities.

71. The quoted market price of an equity security issued to effect a business combination may be used to approximate the fair value of an acquired company if that market price represents fair value (paragraph 65). If, however, the reliability of the quoted market price of stock, either preferred or common, as an indicator of fair value is in doubt (paragraph 24), an estimate of the consideration received is required even though measuring directly the fair values of assets received is difficult. Both the consideration received, including goodwill, and the extent of the adjustment of the quoted market price of the stock issued should be weighed to determine the fair value to be recorded. All aspects of the acquisition, including the negotiations, should be studied, and independent appraisals may be used as an aid in determining the fair value of securities issued. Consideration other than stock distributed to effect an acquisition may provide evidence of the total fair value received.

72. The cost of a company acquired either by disbursing cash or other assets, incurring debt, or issuing stock includes the direct costs of acquisition. However, indirect and general expenses related to acquisitions are deducted as incurred in determining net income.

73. *Controlling interests* — The principles of determining the cost of an acquired company described in paragraphs 69 to 72 also apply to the cost of a controlling interest in a company. A corporation may acquire a controlling interest but not the entire ownership interest of another company. The acquiring corporation should determine a fair value of the acquired company on the same basis as an acquired interest of 100 percent and record the cost of the assets acquired, including goodwill, and liabilities assumed on the basis of that fair value. The minority interest in the acquired company should be reflected at the fair value at the date the corporation acquires control.

74. If a corporation acquires control of another company by purchasing or exchanging securities at various dates, it in effect acquires the other company when the total investment constitutes control and should then account for the acquisition. Investments before control is achieved are classified as intercorporate investments. The fair value of the acquired company should be computed when the investment becomes a controlling interest.

75. *Contingent Consideration.* A business combination agreement may provide for the issuance of additional shares of a security or the transfer of cash or other consideration contingent on · specified events or transactions in the future. Some agreements provide that a portion of the consideration be placed in escrow to be distributed or to be returned to the transferor when specified events occur. Either debt or equity securities may be placed in escrow, and amounts equal to interest or dividends on the securities during the contingency period may be paid to the escrow agent.

76. The Board concludes that the consideration for an acquired company which is recorded at the date of acquisition should be cash and other assets distributed and securities issued unconditionally at that date. Consideration which is issued or issuable at the expiration of the contingency period or which is held in escrow pending the outcome of the contingency should be disclosed but not recorded as a liability or shown as outstanding securities until the outcome of the contingency is determinable beyond reasonable doubt. An issue or distribution of securities or other consideration should then be recorded retroactively as of the date of acquisition and financial statements of intervening periods should be restated appropriately. In general, additional consideration at resolution of contingencies based on earnings should result in an additional element of cost of an acquired company, but additional consideration at resolution of contingencies based on security prices has no effect on the recorded cost of an acquired company.

77. *Contingency based on earnings*—Additional consideration may be contingent on maintaining or achieving specified earnings levels in future periods. On a later date when the earnings level indicates beyond reasonable doubt that additional consideration will be distributable, the acquiring corporation should record the current fair value of the consideration issued or issuable. The cost of the acquired company should be retroactively increased by the amount of the additional consideration, and amortization and depreciation of costs of affected assets should be restated in financial statements presented for prior periods.*

78. *Contingency based on security prices*—Additional consideration may be contingent on the market price of a specified security issued to effect a business combination. Unless the price of the security at least equals the specified amount on a specified date or dates, the acquiring corporation is required to issue additional equity or debt securities or transfer cash or other assets sufficient to make the current fair value of the total consideration equal to the specified amount. The securities issued un-

*This provision effectively amends paragraph 62 of APB Opinion No. 15.

conditionally at the date the combination is consummated should be recorded at that date at the specified amount. On a later date when market prices indicate beyond reasonable doubt that additional consideration will be distributable, the acquiring corporation should record the current fair value of the additional consideration issued or issuable. However, the amount previously recorded for securities issued at the date of acquisition should simultaneously be reduced retroactively to the lower fair value of those securities at the date the additional securities are recorded; the cost of the acquired company is therefore not affected by the contingency provision. Reducing the value of debt securities previously issued to their later fair value results in recording at a discount those debt securities and additional debt securities issued. The discount should be amortized from date the securities are issued, retroactively for the debt securities issued originally.

79. *Interest or dividends during contingency period*—Amounts paid to an escrow agent representing interest and dividends on securities held in escrow should be accounted for according to the accounting for the securities. That is, until the disposition of the securities in escrow is determinable beyond reasonable doubt, payments to the escrow agent should not be recorded as interest expense or dividend distributions. Interest expense and dividends should be recorded retroactively for the prior periods if the escrow securities are distributed later to former stockholders of the acquired company.

80. *Tax effect of imputed interest*—A tax reduction resulting from imputed interest on contingently issuable stock reduces the fair value recorded for contingent consideration based on earnings and increases additional capital recorded for contingent consideration based on security prices.

81. *Compensation in contingent agreements*—The substance of some agreements for contingent consideration is to provide compensation for services or use of property, and the additional consideration given should be accounted for as expenses of the appropriate periods.

82. *Recording Assets Acquired and Liabilities Assumed.* An acquiring corporation should allocate the cost or fair value of an acquired company, determined by applying paragraphs 69 to 81, to the assets acquired and liabilities assumed. Allocation should follow the principles described in paragraph 66.

First, all identifiable assets acquired, either individually or by type, and liabilities assumed in a business combination should be recorded at their fair values at date of acquisition whether or not shown in the financial statements of the acquired company.

Second, the difference between the cost of the acquired company and the sum of the fair values of the identifiable assets acquired less liabilities assumed should be recorded as goodwill. The market or appraisal values of identifiable assets acquired less liabilities assumed may sometimes exceed the cost of the acquired company. If so, the values otherwise assignable to noncurrent assets acquired (except long-term investments in marketable securities) should be reduced by a proportionate part of the excess to determine the fair values; so-called "negative goodwill" should not be recorded unless those assets are reduced to zero value.

Thereafter, assets and liabilities should be accounted for in the same manner as similar assets and liabilities, that is, as receivables, inventories, depreciable assets, liabilities to pay cash, and so forth.

Independent appraisals may be used as an aid in determining the fair values of some assets and liabilities. The effect of taxes should also be considered in assigning fair values to individual assets (paragraph 84).

83. General guides for determining fair values of the individual assets acquired and liabilities assumed, except goodwill, are:

a. Marketable securities at current net realizable values.

b. Claims receivable at present values of amounts to be received determined at appropriate current interest rates, less allowances for uncollectibility and collection costs, if necessary.

c. Inventories:

(1) Finished goods and merchandise at estimated selling prices less the sum of (a) costs of disposal, and (b) a reasonable profit allowance for the selling effort of the acquiring corporation.

(2) Work in process at estimated selling prices of finished goods less the sum of (a) costs to complete, (b) costs of disposal, and (c) a reasonable profit allowance for the completing and selling effort of the acquiring corporation based on profit for similar finished goods.

(3) Raw materials at current replacement costs.

d. Plant and equipment at current replacement costs for similar capacity[12] unless the expected future use of the assets indicates a lower value to the acquirer. Plant and equipment of the acquired company which will be sold or held for later sale rather than used by the acquirer, at current net realizable value.

e. Intangible assets which can be identified and named, including contracts, patents, franchises, customer and supplier lists, and favorable leases, at appraised values.[13]

f. Other assets, including land, natural resources, and non-

marketable securities, at appraised values.

g. Accounts and notes payable, long-term debt, and other claims payable at present values of amounts to be paid determined at appropriate current interest rates.

h. Liabilities and accruals—for example, accruals for pension cost,[14] warranties, vacation pay, deferred compensation—at present values of amounts to be paid determined at appropriate current interest rates.

i. Other liabilities and commitments, including unfavorable leases, contracts, and commitments and plant closing expense incident to the acquisition, at present values of amounts to be paid determined at appropriate current interest rates.

An acquiring corporation does not record as a separate asset the goodwill previously recorded by an acquired company and does not record deferred income taxes recorded by an acquired company before its acquisition. An acquiring corporation should record periodically the accrual of interest on assets and liabilities recorded at acquisition date at the discounted values of amounts to be received or paid.

84. The market or appraisal values of specific assets and liabilities determined in paragraph 83 may differ from the income tax bases of those items. Estimated future tax effects of differences between the tax bases and amounts otherwise appropriate to assign to an asset or a liability are one of the variables in estimating fair value. Amounts assigned as fair values should, for example, recognize that the fair value of an asset to an acquirer is less than its market or

---

[12]Replacement cost may be determined directly if a used asset market exists for the assets acquired. Otherwise, the replacement cost should be approximated from replacement cost new less estimated accumulated depreciation.

[13]Fair values should be ascribed to specific assets; identifiable assets should not be included in goodwill.

[14]An accrual for pension cost should be the greater of (1) the excess, if any, of the actuarially computed value of vested benefits over the amount of the pension fund or (2) accrued pension cost computed in conformity with the accounting policies of the acquiring corporation for one or more of its pension plans.

appraisal value if all or a portion of the market or appraisal value is not deductible for income taxes. The impact of tax effects on fair value depends on numerous factors, including imminence or delay of realization of the asset value and the possible timing of tax consequences. Since differences between fair values and tax bases are not timing differences (APB Opinion No. 11, *Accounting for Income Taxes,* paragraph 13), the acquiring corporation should not record deferred tax accounts at the date of acquisition.

85. The rate-making process for regulated businesses whereby rates are established on a cost-of-service basis (Addendum to APB Opinion No. 2) affects the application of this Opinion. Accordingly, acquired property subject to the regulatory process should be stated at amounts (usually historical original cost at present) which are estimated to be recoverable through depreciation and amortization allowances under the rate-making policies of the applicable rate-regulating agency. The cost of acquired assets, tangible and intangible, recognized under the provisions of this Opinion in excess of the amounts referred to in the preceding sentence should be deferred and charged to income over future periods which may differ from the periods charged for regulatory purposes. The Board expresses neither agreement nor disagreement with property and depreciation bases required or allowed for rate-making purposes.

86. *Acquisition Date.* The statement of income of an acquiring corporation for the period in which a business combination occurs should include income of the acquired company after the date of acquisition by including the revenue and expenses of the acquired operations based on the cost to the acquiring corporation. The Board believes that the date of acquisition of a company should ordinarily be the closing date of a business combination, the date assets are received and other assets are given or stock is issued. The parties may for convenience designate as the effective date the end

of an accounting period between the dates a business combination is announced and closed. The designated date is acceptable for accounting purposes if a written agreement provides that effective control of the acquired company is transferred to the acquiring corporation on that date without restrictions except those required to protect the stockholders or other owners of the acquired company—for example, restrictions on significant changes in the operations until closing, permission to pay dividends equal to those regularly paid before the effective date, and the like.

87. The cost of an acquired company and the fair values of assets acquired and liabilities assumed should be determined as of the acquisition date. If the cost of an acquired company is based on the fair value of securities issued (paragraph 71), their market value for a reasonable period before and after the date the terms of the acquisition are agreed to and announced should be considered.

88. *Disclosure in Financial Statements.* Notes to the financial statements of the acquiring corporation for the period in which a business combination occurs should include the following:

a. Name and a brief description of the acquired company.

b. Method of accounting for the combination—that is, by the purchase method.

c. Period for which results of operations of acquired company are included in the income statement of the acquiring corporation.

d. Cost of acquired company and, if applicable, the number of shares of stock issued or issuable and the amount assigned to the issued and issuable shares.

e. Description of the plan for amortization of acquired goodwill, the amortization method, and period.

f. Contingent payments, options, or commitments specified in the acquisition agreement and

their proposed accounting treatment.

Information relating to several relatively minor acquisitions may be combined for disclosure.

89. Notes to the financial statements of the acquiring corporation for the period in which a business combination occurs should include as supplemental information the following results of operations on a pro forma basis:

a. Results of operations for the current period as though the companies had combined at the beginning of the period, unless the acquisition was at or near the beginning of the period.

b. Results of operations for the immediate preceding period as though the companies had combined at the beginning of that period if comparative financial statements are presented.

The supplemental pro forma information should as a minimum show revenue, income before extraordinary items, net income, and earnings per share. To present pro forma information, income taxes, interest expense, preferred stock dividends, depreciation and amortization of assets, including goodwill, should be adjusted to their accounting bases recognized in recording the combination. Pro forma presentation of results of operations of periods prior to the combination transaction should be limited to the immediate preceding period.

INTANGIBLE ASSETS

Nature of Intangible Assets

90. Accounting for an intangible asset involves the same kinds of problems as accounting for other long-lived assets, namely, determining an initial carrying amount, accounting for that amount after acquisition under normal business conditions (amortization), and accounting for that amount if the value declines substantially and permanently. Solving the problems

is complicated by the characteristics of an intangible asset: its lack of physical qualities makes evidence of its existence elusive, its value is often difficult to estimate, and its useful life may be indeterminable.

91. Various intangible assets differ in their characteristics, their useful lives, their relations to operations, and their later dispositions. Intangible assets may be classified on several different bases:

Identifiability—separately identifiable or lacking specific identification.

Manner of acquisition—acquired singly, in groups, or in business combinations or developed internally.

Expected period of benefit—limited by law or contract, related to human or economic factors, or indefinite or indeterminant duration.

Separability from an entire enterprise — rights transferable without title, salable, or inseparable from the enterprise or a substantial part of it.

Present Accounting for Intangible Assets

92. *Accounting for Costs at Acquisition.* Present principles of accounting for intangible assets are generally similar to those for tangible, long-lived assets such as property, plant, and equipment. Intangible assets acquired from other entities are recorded at cost when acquired. Costs incurred to develop specifically identifiable intangible assets are often recorded as assets if the periods of expected future benefit are reasonably determinable. Costs of developing other intangible assets are usually recorded as expenses when incurred.

93. *Accounting for Deferred Costs After Acquisition.* Intangible assets have been divided into two classes for purposes of accounting for their costs: (a) those with a determinable term of existence because it is limited by law, regulation, or agreement, or by the nature of the asset, and (b) those having no limited term of existence and no

indication of limited life at the time of acquisition. The cost of a type (a) intangible asset is amortized by systematic charges to income over the term of existence or other period expected to be benefited. The cost of a type (b) intangible asset may be treated in either of two ways: (1) the cost may be retained until a limit on the term of existence or a loss of value is evident, at which time the cost is amortized systematically over the estimated remaining term of existence or, if worthless, written off as an extraordinary item in the income statement, or (2) the cost may be amortized at the discretion of management by charges to income even though no present evidence points to a limited term of existence or a loss of value. The cost of an intangible asset may not be written off as a lump sum to capital surplus or to retained earnings (ARB No. 43, Chapter 5 and APB Opinion No. 9).

Basis for Conclusions

94. *Cost of Intangible Assets.* Accounting for the costs that a corporation incurs to develop identifiable intangible assets is beyond the scope of this Opinion. Certain of those costs, for example, research and development costs and preoperating costs, present unusual accounting problems which need to be studied separately. The costs of developing goodwill and other intangible assets with indeterminate lives are ordinarily not distinguishable from the current costs of operations and are thus not assignable to specific assets.

95. Ascertaining the cost of intangible assets acquired either singly or in groups, including intangible assets acquired in a business combination, from other businesses or individuals is discussed in paragraphs 64 to 67 and 69 to 85.

96. *Treatment of Costs.* Costs of intangible assets which have fixed or reasonably determinable terms of existence are now amortized by systematic charges to income over their terms of existence. Differences of opinion center on the amortization of acquired intangible

assets with lives which cannot be estimated reliably either at the date of acquisition or perhaps long after, for example, goodwill and trade names.

97. The literature on business combinations and goodwill, including Accounting Research Study No. 10, *Accounting for Goodwill,* contains at least four possible accounting treatments of goodwill and similar intangible assets:

a. Retain the cost as an asset indefinitely unless a reduction in its value becomes evident.

b. Retain the cost as an asset but permit amortization as an operating expense over an arbitrary period.

c. Retain the cost as an asset but require amortization as an operating expense over its estimated limited life or over an arbitrary but specified maximum and minimum period.

d. Deduct the cost from stockholders' equity at the date acquired.

98. *Arguments for nonamortization*—The two of the four accounting proposals which do not involve amortization of goodwill as an operating expense are based in part on the contention that goodwill value is not consumed or used to produce earnings in the same manner as various property rights and therefore net income should not be reduced by amortization of goodwill. Further, net income should not be reduced by both amortization of goodwill and current expenditures that are incurred to enhance or maintain the value of the acquired intangible assets. All methods of amortizing goodwill are criticized as arbitrary because the life of goodwill is indefinite and an estimated period of existence is not measurable. The basis for proposing that the cost of goodwill be retained as an asset until a loss in value becomes evident is that the cost incurred for acquired goodwill should be accounted for as an asset at the date acquired and in later periods and the cost should not be reduced as long as the value of the

asset is at least equal to that cost. The basis for proposing that the cost of goodwill be deducted from stockholders' equity at the date acquired is that the nature of goodwill differs from other assets and warrants special accounting treatment. Since goodwill attaches only to a business as a whole and its value fluctuates widely for innumerable reasons, estimates of either the terms of existence or current value are unreliable for purposes of income determination.

99. *Accounting on the Historical-Cost Basis.* All assets which are represented by deferred costs are essentially alike in historical-cost based accounting. They result from expenditures or owners' contributions and are expected to increase revenue or reduce costs to be incurred in future periods. If future benefit or the period to be benefited is questionable, the expenditure is usually treated as a current expense and not as a deferred cost. Associating deferred costs with the revenue or period to which they are expected to relate is a basic problem in historical-cost based accounting both in measuring periodic income and in accounting for assets. The basic accounting treatment does not depend on whether the asset is a building, a piece of equipment, an element of inventory, a prepaid insurance premium, or whether it is tangible or intangible. The cost of goodwill and similar intangible assets is therefore essentially the same as the cost of land, buildings, or equipment under historical-cost based accounting. Deducting the cost of an asset from stockholders' equity (either retained earnings or capital surplus) at the date incurred does not match costs with revenue.

100. Accounting for the cost of a long-lived asset after acquisition normally depends on its estimated life. The cost of assets with perpetual existence, such as land, is carried forward as an asset without amortization, and the cost of assets with finite lives is amortized by systematic charges to income. Goodwill and similar intangible assets do not clearly fit either classification; their lives are neither infinite nor specifically limited, but are indeterminate. Thus, although the principles underlying present practice (paragraphs 92 and 93) conform to the principles of accounting for similar types of assets, their applications have led to alternative treatments. Amortizing the cost of goodwill and similar intangible assets on arbitrary bases in the absence of evidence of limited lives or decreased values may recognize expenses and decreases of assets prematurely, but delaying amortization of the cost until a loss is evident may recognize the decreases after the fact.

101. *A Practical Solution.* A solution to this dilemma is to set minimum and maximum amortization periods. This accounting follows from the observation that few, if any, intangible assets last forever, although some may seem to last almost indefinitely. Allocating the cost of goodwill or other intangible assets with an indeterminate life over time is necessary because the value almost inevitably becomes zero at some future date. Since the date at which the value becomes zero is indeterminate, the end of the useful life must necessarily be set arbitrarily at some point or within some range of time for accounting purposes.

Opinion

102. *Acquisition of Intangible Assets.* The Board concludes that a corporation should record as assets the costs of intangible assets acquired from other enterprises or individuals. The costs of developing an identifiable intangible asset may be recorded as an asset, but costs of developing, maintaining, or restoring intangible assets which are not specifically identifiable, have indeterminate lives, or are inherent in a continuing business and related to an enterprise as a whole — such as goodwill — should be deducted from income when incurred.

103. Individual intangible assets should be segregated by their nature, and the cost of each identifiable asset and acquired goodwill should be recorded separately.

a. The cost of an intangible asset or a group of intangible assets acquired in a separate purchase should be determined by the principles described in paragraphs 64 to 67.

b. The costs of identifiable intangible assets acquired in a business combination should be determined by allocating the cost of the acquired company as described in paragraphs 82 to 87.

c. The portion of the cost of an acquired company not allocated to tangible assets, identifiable intangible assets, and liabilities should be designated as the cost of goodwill (paragraph 82).

The same principles determine the cost of goodwill acquired even though a corporation acquires a controlling interest in a company but not the entire ownership interest (paragraphs 73 and 74).

104. *Amortization of Intangible Assets.* The Board believes that the value of intangible assets at any one date eventually disappears and that the recorded costs of intangible assets should be amortized by systematic charges to income over the periods estimated to be benefited. Factors which should be considered in estimating the useful lives of intangible assets include:

a. Legal, regulatory, or contractual provisions may limit the maximum useful life.

b. Provisions for renewal or extension may alter a specified limit on useful life.

c. Effects of obsolescence, demand, competition, and other economic factors may reduce a useful life.

d. A useful life may parallel the service life expectancies of individuals or groups of employees.

e. Expected actions of competitors and others may restrict present competitive advantages.

f. An apparently unlimited useful life may in fact be indefinite and benefits cannot be reasonably projected.

g. An intangible asset may be a composite of many individual factors with varying effective lives.

The method of amortization of intangible assets should be determined from the related factors and the periodic amortization should be reasonable.

105. The Board concludes that the straight-line method of amortization of equal annual amounts should be applied unless a corporation demonstrates that another systematic method is more appropriate. The financial statements should disclose the method and period of amortization. Amortization of acquired goodwill and of other acquired intangible assets not deductible in computing income taxes payable does not create a timing difference, and allocation of income taxes is inappropriate.

106. The cost of each type of intangible asset should be amortized on the basis of the estimated life of that specific asset and should not be written off in the period of acquisition. Analysis of all factors should result in a reasonable estimate of the useful life of most intangible assets. A reasonable estimate of the useful life may often be based on upper and lower limits even though a fixed existence is not determinable. The period of amortization should not, however, exceed forty years. Analysis at the time of acquisition may indicate that the indeterminate lives of some intangible assets are likely to exceed forty years and the cost of those assets should be amortized over the maximum period of forty years, not an arbitrary shorter period.

107. A corporation should evaluate the periods of amortization continually to determine whether later events and circumstances warrant revised estimates of useful lives. If estimates are changed, the unamortized cost should be allocated to the increased or reduced number of remaining periods in the revised useful life but not to exceed forty years after acquisition. Estimation of value and future benefits of an intangible asset may indicate that the unamortized cost should be reduced significantly by a deduction in determining net income (APB Opinion No. 9, paragraph 21). However, a single loss year, or even a few loss years together, does not necessarily justify an extraordinary charge to income for all or a large part of the unamortized cost of intangible assets.

108. *Excess of Acquired Net Assets Over Cost.* The value assigned to net assets acquired should not exceed the cost of an acquired company because the general presumption in historical-cost based accounting is that net assets acquired should be recorded at not more than their cost. The total market or appraisal values of identifiable assets acquired less liabilities assumed in a few business combinations may exceed the cost of the acquired company. An excess over cost should be allocated to reduce proportionately the values assigned to noncurrent assets (except long-term investments in marketable securities) in determining their fair values (paragraph 82). If the allocation reduces the noncurrent assets to zero value, the remainder of the excess over cost should be classified as a deferred credit and should be amortized systematically to income over the period estimated to be benefited but not in excess of forty years. The method and period of amortization should be disclosed. No part of the excess of acquired net assets over cost should be added directly to stockholders' equity at the date of acquisition.

109. *Disposal of Goodwill.* Ordinarily goodwill and similar intangible assets cannot be disposed of separately from the enterprise as a whole. An acquired company or large segment of it may, however, subsequently be sold or otherwise liquidated, and all or a portion of the unamortized cost of the goodwill recognized in the acquisition should be included in the cost of the assets sold.

EFFECTIVE DATE

110. The provisions of this Opinion shall be effective to account for business combinations initiated after June 30, 1970 and intangible assets recognized in those business combinations or otherwise acquired after June 30, 1970. Business combinations initiated before June 30, 1970 and consummated after that date under the original terms may be accounted for in accordance with this Opinion or the applicable previous pronouncements of the Board and its predecessor committee.

111. The provisions of this Opinion should not be applied retroactively for business combinations consummated before June 30, 1970 or to intangible assets acquired before June 30, 1970, whether in those business combinations or otherwise.

112. The Board encourages the application on a prospective basis to all intangible assets held on June 30, 1970 of the provision in paragraphs 104 to 107 of this Opinion which requires amortization of all intangible asets over the periods described.

113. If a corporation holds as an investment on March 1, 1970 a minority interest in the common stock of another company and the corporation initiates after June 30, 1970 a plan of combination with that company, the resulting business combination may be accounted for by the pooling of interests method providing

the combination is completed within five years after June 30, 1970 and

the combination meets all conditions specified in paragraphs 44 to 47, except that

the corporation which effects the combination issues common stock for at least 90 percent of the outstanding common stock interest, as described in paragraph 46(b), of the other combining company not already held at March 1, 1970 (rather than 90 percent of all of the common stock interest of the combining company).[15]

---

[15]The exception does not affect the measure of relative size described in paragraph 45(b).

The investment in common stock held on March 1, 1970 should not be accounted for as treasury stock or retired stock at the date of the combination. Instead, the excess of cost over the investor corporation's proportionate equity in the net assets of the combining company at or near the date the stock investment was acquired should be allocated to identifiable assets of the combining company at the date the combination is consummated on the basis of the fair values of those assets at the combination date. The unallocated portion of the excess should be assigned to an unidentified intangible asset (goodwill) and should be accounted for according to applicable previous pronouncements of the Board and its predecessor committee. The cost of goodwill should not be amortized retroactively but may be amortized prospectively under the provision of paragraph 112. If the cost of the investment is less than the investor's equity in the net assets of the combining company, that difference should reduce proportionately the recorded amounts of noncurrent assets (except long-term investments in marketable securities) of the combining company.

NOTES

Opinions of the Accounting Principles Board present the conclusions of at least two-thirds of the members of the Board, which is the senior technical body of the Institute authorized to issue pronouncements on accounting principles. Council of the Institute has resolved that Institute members should disclose departures from Board Opinions in their reports as independent auditors when the effect of the departures on the financial statements is material or see to it that such departures are disclosed in notes to the financial statements and, where practicable, should disclose their effects on the financial statements (Special Bulletin, *"Disclosure of Departures from Opinions of the Accounting Principles Board,"* October 1964). Members of the Institute must assume the burden of justifying any such departures.

Covering all possible conditions and circumstances in an Opinion of the Accounting Principles Board is usually impracticable. The substance of transactions and the principles, guides, rules, and criteria described in Opinions should control the accounting for transactions not expressly covered.

Unless otherwise stated, Opinions of the Board are not intended to be retroactive. They are not intended to be applicable to immaterial items.

Index